PRINTED MAPS OF UTAH TO 1900

Printed Maps of Utah to 1900:

An Annotated Cartobibliography

by

Riley Moore Moffat

Western Association of Map Libraries

Occasional Paper No. 8   1981

Library of Congress Cataloging in Publication Data

Moffat, Riley Moore, 1947-
    Printed maps of Utah to 1900.

    (Occasional paper - Western Association of
Map Libraries ; no. 8)
    Originally presented as the author's thesis
(M.A.), Brigham Young University, 1980.
    Includes index.
    1. Utah--Maps--Bibliography. I. Title.
II. Series: Western Association of Map Libraries.
Occasional paper ; no. 8.
Z6027.U5M74 1981 [GA453]   016.912'792   81-659
                                             AACR1

            ISBN 0-939112-09-4

Information regarding this series and other
publications of WAML may be found on page 177.

Table of Contents

List of Figures

MAP ON COVER

Map of the Settlements in the Great Salt Lake Country. Utah.
Described in Entry 87 on page 74.

Foreword

The Publications Committee of the Western Association of Map Libraries is particularly pleased that Riley Moffat, Map Librarian at Brigham Young University, offered his Master's Thesis to WAML for consideration as an Occasional Paper. Although the Occasional Paper series has not been restricted to works about the Western North America region, it is an expressed hope that Members of the Association would be encouraged to author such works and make this series their first choice as a vehicle for presentation of those works to the WAML audience.

We believe *Printed Maps of Utah to 1900* is unique in the field of cartobibliographies, and we expect it to become a standard reference work.

Printed Maps of Utah to 1900: An Annotated Cartobibliography, as a Thesis, was presented by Mr. Moffat to the Department of Geography, Brigham Young University, in partial fulfillment of the requirements for his Master of Science degree. Professors Robert L. Layton and Richard H. Jackson, to whom the Thesis was presented in August, 1980, served as faculty advisors. It is published here in its entirety, with the following modification: Chapter I and the Bibliography have been revised (as submitted by Mr. Moffat for an article to the Utah Historical Quarterly).

We are indebted to members of the Publications Committee for their editorial judgment: R. Philip Hoehn (Chairman), Ronald Whistance-Smith, and Charles A. Seavey. The Committee is grateful to the WAML Executive Committee for support of its recommendation to publish: David A. Lundquist (President), Barbara Cox (Vice-President), Rosanna Miller (Secretary).

I would especially like to thank Phil Hoehn for his assistance in my preparation of the typescript for publication.

Stanley D. Stevens
Editor of Publications
Western Association of Map Libraries

Acknowledgements

I wish to acknowledge the assistance of my colleagues, Chad Flake and Scott Duval of Brigham Young University, Susan Mortenson of the Utah State Historical Society, Ruth Yeaman of the University of Utah, Karlo Mustonen and Steve Weiss of Utah State University, Inez Cooper of Southern Utah State College, David Putnam of the Genealogical Society, Richard Stephenson of the Library of Congress, Grant Anderson and Earl Olsen of the L.D.S. Church Historical Department for opening their collections to me, and for their general encouragement. The support and encouragement of the Geography Department faculty and the Harold B. Lee Library Administration is greatly appreciated. I would also like to express my appreciation to my wife, Connie, for supporting this project through to completion and Bonnie Percival and Valerie Clark for their typing.

Provo, Utah   Riley Moffat
August 1980

Preface

This cartobibliography has been prepared to serve as a reference and research guide and to provide a convenient means of locating and identifying nineteenth century printed maps of Utah. Old maps are useful historical documents. However, they are often hard to find, time and abuse having taken their toll, and when found they are sometimes difficult to identify.

This cartobibliography will deal with printed maps of Utah published before 1900. The year 1900 was set as the cut-off date to avoid many mass-produced maps, to somewhat coincide with the creation of the State of Utah, and to close the decade which saw Utah adequately surveyed. A major question which had to be considered was where to set the limit on maps which show Utah as well as adjoining areas, territories, or states. No hard and fast rule could be devised, though date and scale were factors. The older the map, the more leeway was allowed to show Utah in its geographical setting. Also the older the map, a smaller minimum scale was allowed, varying from about 1:7,000,000 for early maps to about 1:3,000,000 for newer maps.

In compiling this cartobibliography, all available published lists were consulted and references to them given in each entry. Part of this project parallels Mapping the Transmississippi West, the five volume tour de force of Carl I. Wheat. The map citations

in the Introduction refer to these volumes. However, Wheat's
work is limited to regional maps and ceases comprehensive coverage
about 1869.

All known collections of early Utah maps were sought out
and visited. The following collections were surveyed personally
and all relevant maps and atlases examined: (1) Brigham Young
University, Lee Library, Provo; (2) The Church of Jesus Christ of
Latter-Day Saints, Historical Department, Salt Lake City; (3) The
Genealogical Society of Utah, Salt Lake City; (4) Provo Public
Library, Provo; (5) Salt Lake City Public Library, Salt Lake
City; (6) Snow College Library, Ephraim; (7) Southern Utah State
College Library, Cedar City; (8) University of Utah, Marriott
Library, Salt Lake City; (9) Utah State Archives, Salt Lake City;
(10) Utah State Historical Society, Salt Lake City; (11) Utah
State University, Merrill Library, Logan; (12) Weber County
Library, Ogden; and (13) Weber State College Library, Ogden. Other
libraries were queried by mail: Logan Public Library, Brigham
City Public Library, Davis County Library, Salt Lake County
Library, Tooele Public Library, American Fork Public Library,
Springville Public Library, Price Public Library, College of
Eastern Utah Library, Vernal Public Library, Moab Public Library,
Richfield Public Library, Cedar City Public Library, St. George
Public Library, and Dixie College Library. None of these libraries
indicated they had collections of nineteenth century printed maps
of Utah.

Maps appearing in atlases and selected books have been
included and an effort made to identify the source of those used.
Unfortunately, it is the practice of many antiquarian book and map
dealers to dismember old atlases and sell the plates individually
for a much greater profit. This often makes establishing the map's
provenance difficult, especially if the publisher, engraver, copyright date, page number, or title is missing.

Dating maps of certain commercial atlas publishers can be
a problem. Often a map is reprinted for years with no revision and
perhaps only a different page number to indicate a different
impression. Also revisions may be made but not indicated in the
copyright information. After about 1850, several United States
atlas publishers began publishing atlases which depict Utah
separately or in conjunction with adjoining territories and states.
The atlases which supply most of the commercially printed maps of
Utah in the second half of the nineteenth century include the
following:

1. A New Universal Atlas by Samuel Augustus Mitchell, 17
editions between 1846 and 1864

2. Atlas of the World by Joseph Hutchins Colton, four
editions between 1854 and 1878

3. Colton's General Atlas by Joseph Hutchins Colton, 22
editions between 1857 and 1888

4. Johnson's New Illustrated (Steel Plate) Family Atlas by
Alvin Jewett Johnson, 21 editions between 1860 and 1886

5. Mitchell's New General Atlas by Samuel Augustus Mitchell,

31 editions between 1860 and 1893

6. Asher & Adams New Commercial, Topographical, and
Statistical Atlas and Gazeteer of the United States, 16 editions
between 1872 and 1875

7. Atlas of the United States by Ormando Willis Gray, 11
editions between 1873 and 1879

8. The National Atlas by Ormando Willis Gray, 30 editions
between 1875 and 1889

9. Rand McNally's Commercial Atlas and Marketing Guide,
published annually since 1876

10. Gaylord Watson published five atlases under various
titles, between 1877 and 1885

11. The Rand McNally & Co.'s Indexed Atlas of the World, 17
editions between 1881 and 1899

12. Cram's Unrivaled Family Atlas of the World by George
Franklin Cram, 14 editions between 1882 and 1891

13. Bradley's Atlas of the World for Commercial and Library
Reference by William M. Bradley, 14 editions between 1885 and 1896

14. Cram's Unrivaled Atlas of the World by George Franklin
Cram, 15 editions between 1887 and 1899[1]

The entries in the cartobibliography are arranged chrono-
logically by date of publication, or occasionally by date of

---

[1] American Library Association, Resources and Technical
Service Division, The National Union Catalog; Pre-1956 Imprints
(London: Mansel, 1968-   ).

information if it differs significantly from the printed copyright date. The title is given as it appears on the face of the map. The size of the map is given in centimeters, from inside the neat lines, vertical first then horizontal. Distinguishing features, peculiarities, inaccuracies, and general description is given to help identify the map. The provenance of the map and its citations in other lists are given, including atlas and book titles, Congressional report numbers, Serial Set numbers, and Superintendent of Documents call numbers. Sources of the citations can be found in the bibliography. Last is given the collections in Utah which hold a copy of the map, either in original form or permanent photographic reproduction. Location symbols used are as follows:

BL: University of California, Bancroft Library, Berkeley.

BYU: Brigham Young University, Lee Library, Provo.

LDSH: The Church of Jesus Christ of Latter-Day Saints Historical Department Library, Salt Lake City.

GSL: Genealogical Society of Utah Library, Salt Lake City.

LC: Library of Congress, Geography and Map Division, Washington.

SLP: Salt Lake City Public Library, Special Collections, Salt Lake City.

SUS: Southern Utah State College Library, Special Collections, Cedar City.

UU: University of Utah, Marriott Library, Western Americana, Salt Lake City.

UHS: Utah State Historical Society, Salt Lake City

USU: Utah State University, Merrill Library, Special

        Collections, Logan.

WCL: Weber County Library, Special Collections, Ogden.

Chapter I

Introduction

Although the first map of Utah from actual observation was not made until 1777, cartographers had been conjecturing about the geography of the interior of western North America, with some degree of accuracy, since the first penetrations in the 1530's and 1540's. Information from these expeditions led cartographers to believe that the region now encompassing Utah was mountainous with a large river flowing out of the north and emptying into the Gulf of California. This river, now known as the Colorado, was called Tontonteanch or Tototeac by Fray Marcos de Niza and began appearing on maps as early as 1546. This concept of the interior of western North America is illustrated by the 1566 map of Bolognino Zaltieri (Map 12 in Carl I. Wheat's Mapping the Transmississippi West).

In 1583, Antonio de Espejo visited the Rio Grande pueblos of New Mexico and the Hopi villages of Arizona. There he heard of a large lake to the north which began appearing on maps as early as Richard Hakluyt's New World Map of 1587 (Wheat 21). Nothing new was learned of western North America in the seventeenth century, and perceptions of it regressed with the notion that California was an island. Such eminent cartographers as Henry Briggs, Jan Jansson,

1

and Nicolas Sanson portray Espejo's mythical lake as being drained by the Rio Grande de Norte into the Gulf of California.

Baron Louis de Lahontan visited the Mississippi Valley at the end of the seventeenth century and there heard of a large salt lake to the west which he reported in 1703. A trained engineer, Francisco Alvarez y Barreiro, toured the Spanish northern frontier from 1724 to 1728 with Don Pedro de Rivera. On his map of 1728 (Wheat 115) the "R. Colorado" and "R. Azul" are tributaries of the "Rio de Xila". The mythical lake to the north is drained by the "R. Azul" which flows south to the east of the "R. Colorado". But more interesting is his note printed on the map west of the lake that the area is believed to have been the homeland of "los Indios Mexicanos". This fanciful belief was noted on subsequent maps down to Fremont's time, including the maps of Miera and Humboldt. The 1768 map of Jose Antonio de Alzate y Ramirez (Wheat 149) includes the note regarding the Indians destined for Mexico on the eastern side of the lake. He calls the lake "Laguna de Teguayo", does not show any outlet for it, and wisely disclaims knowledge of the course of any rivers of that region.

After the settlement of California commenced, it became important for the Spanish to establish a land route from Santa Fe to Monterey. To this end, Fray Francisco Atanasio Dominguez, Fray Silvestre Velez de Escalante, and a party of ten left Santa Fe for Monterey on July 29, 1776. The Dominguez-Escalante expedition was a failure in that it did not succeed in reaching Monterey. However, the expedition is much better known for being the first Europeans

of record to venture into what is today known as Utah. With the
party was an experienced cartographer and military engineer, Captain
Bernardo de Miera y Pacheco. On returning to Santa Fe on January 2,
1777, Miera drew a map to accompany Escalante's Diario Derrotero
(Wheat 173, 174, 176, 177, 178, 179). Originally only in manuscript
form, it has since been printed and must be considered the genesis
of Utah cartography. Although Miera spent two of the expedition's
five months traveling in Utah, his map still sired several misconceptions about the geography of the region which were to haunt map
makers for sixty to eighty years. Miera's "Rio de S. Buenaventura"
(Green River) flows into "Laguna Miera" (Sevier Lake) rather than
into the "Rio Zaguaganas" (Colorado River). He also showed a large,
unnamed river flowing west out of the larger northern lobe of "Laguna de los Timpanogos" (the Great Salt Lake and Utah Lake combined
and connected by a narrow strait). The map was hand copied several
times with few minor geographical changes, but with significant
changes in illustrative materials by which each is distinguished.

No new or better information about Utah appeared on maps
until the 1830's when information supplied by Jedediah Strong Smith
became available to a few cartographers. Even the discoveries of
the Dominguez-Escalante expedition might not have been known outside of Spanish circles had not Alexander von Humboldt had access
to a Miera map, or a map based on his information. Although it is
not certain that Humboldt used a copy of the Miera map, in constructing his 1804 map of New Spain (Wheat 272), he did have access to
the Miguel Costansó map of 1779 (Wheat 182), the Manuel Mascaró map

of 1782 (Wheat 193), and possibly the "La Paz" map of 1783 (Wheat 195) which all used Miera's geography for their Utah portions. The "La Paz" map extended the Rio de San Buenaventura to San Francisco Bay and is probably based on information received from Father Francisco Garces after listening to Indian tales in the San Joaquin Valley.

Mythical rivers continued to drain Utah and the Great Basin to the Pacific coast until Fremont's time. On Dr. John Hamilton Robinson's map of 1819 (Wheat 334), the Laguna Timpanogos (Great Salt Lake) is drained by the River Timpanogos into San Francisco Bay, while the Rio de San Buenaventura drains a smaller, unnamed lake to the south (Laguna de Miera, or Sevier Lake) to the coast at Mission San Antonio. Also on Robinson's map is depicted the "Multomah River" (Willamette River) as rising in the area of the Raft River Range northwest of the Great Salt Lake and flowing to the Columbia at Fort Vancouver, a notion of the Lewis and Clark expedition. The 1821 map of the French Royal Geographer, Alexandre Emile Lapie (Wheat 342), includes information from the Astorians which shows a "Millers River" (Bear River) for the first time on a reasonably accurate course. Lapie's "Lac Timpanogos" is drained by another "Riv. Miller" to the Pacific coast north of San Francisco, and his "L. Teguayo" (Sevier Lake) is drained by an unnamed river into San Francisco Bay.

Henry Schenck Tanner's 1822 map of North America (Wheat 350) shows ever more fantastic Great Basin geography. Lake Timpanogos is drained by two rivers to the Pacific, the familiar "R. Timpanogos" flowing into San Francisco Bay and a new "Los Mongos R." flowing into the Pacific at Point Orford. Tanner's "Salt Lake" (Sevier Lake) is fed by two river systems from the east and northeast, the "R. de S. Buenaventura" and the "Rio Salado", and is drained by the "R. S. Buenaventura" to the Pacific at "S. Antonio" as on Robinson's map. A note on the map cautiously qualifies this information:

> *The information respecting the interior of new California whence the Rivers Los Mongos, Timpanogos & S. Buenaventura where traced on this map: was not of that authentic character which distinguished nearly all the other materials used in its construction; it is therefore very doubtful whether the representation afforded by it of the courses and magnitude of those streams should be relied on as correct.*[1]

The Fur Trappers

An accurate picture of the geography of Utah and the Great Basin was dealt a severe blow by the untimely death of Jedediah Strong Smith in 1831. Smith explored Utah from 1824 to 1827 as a fur trapper. He crossed the South Pass and the Green River in 1824 calling it the "Seedskeeder". In 1826, he traversed Utah from Cache Valley to the mouth of the Virgin River and there recognized the Colorado as the "Seedskeeder". This corrected Miera's idea that the Green River, his "Rio de San Buenaventura", drained into Sevier Lake, his "Laguna de Miera". In 1827, Smith crossed the Great Basin from Walker Lake to Cache Valley, then retraced his route southwestward to the Mohave villages. Later that year

---

[1] Wheat, Carl Irving. Mapping the Transmississippi West. 5 vols. in 6. Vol. 2:84. San Francisco: The Institute of Historical Cartography, 1957-63.

traveling up what he considered the Buenaventura (Sacramento River), he determined that it did not drain the Great Salt Lake. Back in St. Louis in 1830, he hired Samuel Parkinson to assist him with publishing his journal and map. Smith was killed May 27, 1831, by Comanche Indians while on a trip to Santa Fe, his map and book unpublished. The existence today of any maps he drew is unknown. That he did draw some manuscript maps is evidenced by the detailed cartography credited to him which fell into the hands of a select few mapmakers. The fact that his journal and map were not publish-ed and disseminated, left most geographers unsure of the interior West until Fremont's time.

> Everywhere he touched his pencil, west of the continental divide, Jedediah made cartographic news. At long last he got the facts straight about the Great Salt Lake, showing its self-con-tained drainage basin, with such features as the Bear River, Bear Lake, the Weber River, and the dependent relations of Utah Lake all made clear. To the south, the Sevier River and Lake, the Bea-ver River and the Virgin River were all correctly depicted in relation one to the other, and to the general character of the drainage. Miera in 1776 had seen most of these physiographic features but had possessed insufficient background and infor-mation to interpret them as a whole, and time and fantasy had wrought wonders with the facts that Escalante brought back from his entrada into the Great Basin.[2]

Other trappers and traders were in Utah during these years. Mauricio Arze and Lagos Garcia traveled from Santa Fe in 1813. Peter Skene Ogden, Jim Bridger, and Etienne Provost trapped in northern Utah in 1824-26. James Ohio Pattie claimed to have trav-

---

[2] *Ibid.*, 2:134.

eled from the Grand Canyon to the South Pass in 1826. Richard
Campbell, Antonio Armijo, and William Wolfskill claimed to have
traveled the Spanish Trail from Santa Fe to Los Angeles in 1827,
1829, and 1830 respectively. Unfortunately, none of these people,
with the exception of Ogden, left any maps.

Another French Royal Geographer, Adrien Hubert Brué, was
the first to use information derived from Smith's explorations on
his maps of Mexico, published in 1833 and 1834 (Wheat 401 and 404).
They are based on a Smith letter, not a map, and are very incom-
plete. Peter Skene Ogden, who had met Smith in the Far West, supplied information to Aaron Arrowsmith for his Map of British North
America in 1834 (Wheat 403). Albert Gallatin's little known Map
of the Indian Tribes of North America (Wheat 417) in 1836 was the
most accurate yet, showing Smith's geography and routes without the
hinderance of any mythical preconceptions. Also in 1836, H. S.
Tanner used Smith information to correct the fantastic geography
he displayed on his 1822 map of North America. Another fur trapper, Warren Angus Ferris, drew a map in 1836 (Wheat 416) which, in
its amateurish fashion, depicts the relationship of Utah's hydro-
graphic features with even more accuracy. Unfortunately, this manuscript map was unavailable to the cartographers of the time and
only came to light in 1940.

Smith's explorations are cartographically culminated in
David H. Burr's 1839 Map of the United States (Wheat 411). Dale
L. Morgan and Carl I. Wheat believed Burr's accuracy is based on
the fact that he had access to a map Smith drew for General

William H. Ashley, a former employer of Smith's. As a United States Congressman from Missouri from 1831 to 1837, Ashley came in contact with Burr, who was then Geographer to the House of Representatives.[3] Burr's involvement with Utah is significant. After publishing his Atlas of New York in 1829, which is important to Mormon church history, he became in 1832 Topographer to the Post Office Department and Geographer to the House of Representatives. In 1855, Burr received his last position, that of United States Surveyor-General of Utah Territory, retiring in 1858 as an invalid.

In 1953, Wheat found a copy of Fremont's 1845 map on which George Gibbs had drawn Smith's routes and geography while in Oregon in 1851 (Wheat 398). Gibbs wrote in his journal that Smith's map, which he had apparently drawn while at Fort Vancouver in 1827, had been purchased in Oregon by the Joint Commission of Army and Navy Officers and probably taken to Washington, D.C.[4]

About this time a new cartographical myth began that was to plague map makers for over thirty years. Beginning with Tanner in 1836, Bonneville in 1837, and Burr in 1839, a "Lost River" and "Lost Lake", later known as Ashley or Preuss Lake, began appearing south or southwest of Sevier Lake, also known as Ashley's Lake or Nicollett Lake. Dale Morgan believed this came from Smith and Fremont connecting the Beaver River (Lost River) with Little Salt Lake (Lost Lake). By 1848, Lost Lake, or Preuss Lake, had migra-

---

[3] Goetzman, William H. Army Exploration in the American West, 1803-1863. New Haven, CT: Yale University Press, 1959, p.51.

[4] Wheat, 2:129.

ted farther west to the Nevada border until George M. Wheeler found during his expeditions of 1869-1873 that instead of the two lakes only one, Sevier Lake, actually existed.

The Military Explorations

The Corps of Topographical Engineers of the War Department was formed in 1838. One of its main assignments was the mapping of the little known western parts of the country. The first western expedition of the Topographical Engineers was carried out in the years 1842, 1843, and 1844 by John Charles Fremont. This was to be the first organized, scientific mapping effort in the far west, notwithstanding the efforts of earlier United States representatives such as B. L. E. Bonneville in 1837, Washington Hood in 1838, and Charles Wilkes in 1841.

Fremont and his cartographer Charles Preuss approached the Great Salt Lake from the east in 1843, mapped the Bear River to its mouth and the north shore of the Great Salt Lake down to the Weber River, before going on to Oregon. On their way back from Oregon and California in 1844, they passed through Las Vegas and "Vegas de Santa Clara" (Mountain Meadows), then followed the present route of I-15 from Cedar City to Spanish Fork before passing out of the state through the Uintah Basin. Fremont and Preuss accurately mapped their route through Utah showing only those features which they actually saw and leaving the rest blank, with one exception. They somehow showed the Great Salt Lake and Utah Lake as one body of water with a narrow strait existing where the Jordan River should have been. This representation of the Great Salt

Lake and Utah Lake reflects Miera's geography, yet Fremont had

personally surveyed much of the northern and western shores of the

Great Salt Lake and had viewed Utah Lake from the south end of Utah

Valley. What Jedediah Smith had determined eighteen years earlier,

Fremont verified and publicized:

> The map depicting all these travels radically
> and permanently altered western cartography. There
> would appear a few throwbacks of course, but with
> thousands of copies of Fremont's authoritative re-
> port and map in print, no cartographer could find
> reasonable excuse for not fairly representing the
> main features of the West.[5]

Though Fremont indicates in his Memoirs[6] that he was un-

aware of Smith's explorations, Wheat further eulogizes him:

> Fremont is the great authority for the Great
> Basin and appears as the explorer par excellence
> of this region. It was long before any of the com-
> mercial cartographers discovered anything else to
> copy.[7]

It is obvious that maps accurately displaying the main fea-

tures of Utah's geography were available when Brigham Young travel-

ed west with the first company of Mormon pioneers in 1847. Young

and his associates had with them Fremont's map of 1845 which Wil-

lard Richards and William Clayton regularly annotated to show the

company's progress and observations along the trail. They also had

Samuel Augustus Mitchell's 1846 edition of A New Map of Texas, Or-

egon, and California, which follows Fremont's geography and of

---

[5] *Ibid.*, 2:199.

[6] Fremont, John Charles. Memoirs of My Life. Chicago:
     Bedford, Clarke & Co., 1887, p. 432.

[7] Wheat, 3:150.

which Brigham Young had ordered a half dozen copies from Joseph A. Stratton in St. Louis. While Fremont was again out adventuring in California, Charles Preuss stayed in the East and published a detailed strip map in 1846 of the Oregon Trail in seven sheets, a copy of which was sent to Brigham Young at Winter Quarters by Thomas L. Kane.[8]

The discovery of gold sparked intense new interest in the West. Many new maps appeared. The better ones used Fremont as their authority for the Utah portions. In 1848, Fremont and Preuss came out with a new edition of their map of the West with much new information, including a correction of the relationship of Utah Lake to the Great Salt Lake.

Another officer of the Topographical Engineers, Captain Howard Stansbury, was assigned to make a topographical examination of the Great Salt Lake. Stansbury completed his detailed survey of the Wasatch Front and Great Salt Lake during the seasons of 1849 and 1850, but the maps were not published until 1852. His correction of the shape of the Great Salt Lake did appear on the important 1850 map of the West by the Topographical Engineers. During this time the term Wasatch Mountains, which Fremont had limited to below the Sevier River in 1844, had migrated north to Spanish Fork in 1848 and was finally extended north to the Bear River by Stansbury in 1852.

---

[8] Jackson, Richard H. Myth and Reality: Environmental Perception of the Mormons, 1840-1865; An Historical Geosophy. (Ph.D. Dissertation.) Worcester, Massachusetts: Clark University, 1970, pp. 105-109.

By 1850, Utah was taking a prominent and recognizable place on the maps and atlases of commercial publishers, especially those of Joseph Hutchins Colton and Samuel Augustus Mitchell. Utah county boundaries began appearing on maps in 1853 when John Disturnell showed eleven counties covering a Utah Territory stretching from Lake Tahoe to the Continental Divide.

The need to improve communications between the East and West coasts provided the impetus for the government in 1853 to fund a series of surveys to locate the most practicable route for a railroad from the Mississippi Valley to the Pacific Coast along different degrees of latitude. Four of the five routes proposed were explored in detail. One of the proposed routes passed through Utah, roughly along the 39th parallel. It was explored by Lt. Edward Griffin Beckwith in 1854 and Captain John Williams Gunnison in 1855. When Captain Gunnison and his topographer Richard H. Kern were killed by Indians near the site of Delta, Beckwith and his topographer F. W. Egloffstein salvaged his notes and completed the maps. These surveys added much new detail to the country approximating the route of the present I-70 from Colorado to the Sevier Valley. This information was incorporated on Major William Hemsley Emory's 1857 general map of the Gadsden Purchase boundary survey and on Lt. Gouveneur Kemble Warren's monumental map of the West in 1857.

When the United States forces under Colonel Albert Sidney Johnston arrived in Utah, Captain James Hervey Simpson was assigned to map out existing and possible wagon roads throughout the territory. His maps show in detail the transportation network of Utah in 1859. Captain Simpson explored many routes and added much detail and many place names across the deserts of western Utah and Nevada. Unfortunately, the Civil War delayed publication of some of his maps until 1876.

In 1859, when Captain John N. Macomb was assigned to explore the area from Santa Fe to the junction of the Grand and Green Rivers, southeastern Utah was basically a blank on the map with only the supposed courses of the Colorado River and some of its real and imaginary tributaries shown. Besides detailing new territory along the route, the map to illustrate the report was drawn using a new technique devised by "Baron" F. W. von Egloffstein. This map and another map to illustrate the explorations of Lt. Joseph C. Ives were drawn on steel plates. Relief is shown by hill shading instead of by hachures. It is to imitate a plaster model, according to Egloffstein. Actually, the shading effect was achieved by drawing extremely fine-ruled lines on the steel plates.[9] Again, because of the Civil War, this map was not published until 1875.

The sum total of the geographical knowledge of Utah at the outset of the Civil War is revealed on the Bureau of Topographical Engineer's map of the Territory and Military Department of Utah. Though dated 1860, it includes information from explorations in 1861. During the Civil War, the military suspended mapping activ-

---

[9] Ives, Joseph Christmas. Report Upon the Colorado River of the West. Washington, D.C.: U.S. Government Printing Office, 1861. Appendix D.

ities in Utah. Although the Surveyor General's Office was active
in mapping other western states and territorities during this time,
it made no map of Utah from 1856 to 1866.

Printed maps of the decade 1861-1870 were basically the do-
main of commercial publishers like Samuel Augustus Mitchell and
Joseph Hutchins Colton, who also supplied maps for Alvin Jewett
Johnson. The first major regional map publisher appeared in 1863
when Hubert Howe Bancroft of San Francisco began publishing large
and detailed wall maps by William H. Knight. Though new editions
of some of these maps were issued faithfully once and even twice
a year, new information was often slow in appearing. An example
of this lag is the tardy depiction of the many changes in Utah's
state and county boundaries between 1861 and 1868. Later in this
decade, the transcontinental railroad was constructed and new editions of the popular maps faithfully show the latest construction
progress. Ironically, the railroad did not follow any of the routes laboriously surveyed in the 1850's.

The year 1869 heralds both the completion of the transcontinental railroad and the arrival of Bernard Arnold Martin Froiseth, Utah's most famous cartographer. B. A. M. Froiseth, as his
name appears on all his maps, came to Salt Lake City from Washington, D.C. in 1869. He published his first map in 1870, or rather
three small maps on one sheet, two dated 1870 and one dated 1869
(Wheat 1222). On this map appears Brigham Young's portrait and his
signed statement, "Correct. Brigham Young." The next year Froiseth
issued a large New Mining Map of Utah . . . showing only the north

central part of the territory from the Tintic District to Logan.
That same year he published the first edition of his monumental
Froiseth's New Sectional & Mineral Map of Utah . . .; a second edi-
tion which added much new information, especially from the J. W.
Powell surveys in southeastern Utah, was printed in 1875. This
second edition was reprinted in 1878 and 1879.

The Great Surveys

Edward Freyhold, who had helped Lt. G. K. Warren on his
landmark map of 1857, drafted a major revision of that map in 1868
(Wheat 1185) which depicted the geographical knowledge of that year.
Large blank spaces still covered many portions of Utah. This was
the situation on the eve of what has become known as the "Great
Western Surveys". These were four separate surveys headed by Clarence King, George Montague Wheeler, Ferdinand Vandiveer Hayden,
and John Wesley Powell. These four government surveys attempted
among other things to fill in those blank spaces on the Warren/
Freyhold map.

The first of the great surveys was Clarence King's "United
States Geological Exploration of the Fortieth Parallel". King's
survey paralleled the transcontinental railroad, and he spent the
seasons of 1868 and 1869 in Utah. Of the five maps published in
both topographic and geologic editions in the 1876 Geological and
Topographic Atlas, two deal with Utah.

The "United States Geographical Surveys West of the One
Hundredth Meridian" of George Montague Wheeler undertook the most
extensive and detailed mapping of Utah. Whereas the other surveys

were interested in natural resources, Lt. Wheeler was more interested in mapping the topography for military purposes. In 1869, Wheeler was assigned to make a thorough reconnaissance of eastern Nevada between the White Pine District and Colorado River, one of the blanks on the Warren/Freyhold map. On December 4, 1871, he proposed mapping the entire region west of the one hundredth meridian at the scale of eight miles to one inch, which was later changed to four miles to an inch. Of the ninety-five quadrangles proposed, mapping was completed in twenty-seven by 1879 when the survey was terminated. The completed sheets were brought together in one folio volume in 1889. Eight of these sheets are in Utah and appear in several different editions showing relief either by hachures or by hill shading and with overprints showing geology or land use (figure 1). Among other things, Wheeler determined that the apocryphal Preuss Lake and Sevier Lake were one and the same. As part of this survey, Grove Karl Gilbert mapped the shoreline of prehistoric Lake Bonneville.

The "United States Geological and Geographical Survey of the Territories" led by Ferdinand Vandiveer Hayden was organized in 1869 and is best known for its explorations and surveying in Colorado and the Yellowstone region, though a few maps do include some Utah Territory.

John Wesley Powell began his "United States Geographical and Geological Survey of the Rocky Mountain Region" in 1869 by descending the Green and Colorado Rivers. No official maps of his river trips were published, though some information from his 1871

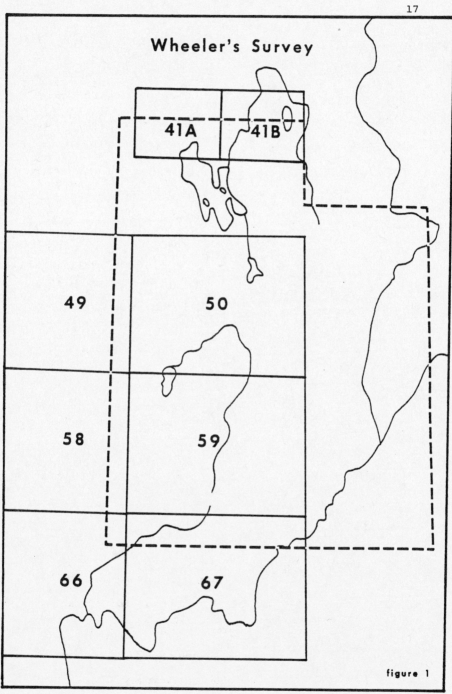

Wheeler's Survey

41A 41B

49 50

58 59

66 67

figure 1

expedition was used in later maps of the Uintah Mountains, the High Plateaus, and the Grand Cañon District. His <u>Report on the Lands of the Arid Region</u> . . . includes a large and important map of Utah detailing potential land usage. Powell's final and cartographically most impressive project was the <u>Topographic and Geologic Atlas of the District or the High Plateaus of Utah to Accompany the Report of Captain C. E. Dutton</u>. These maps exhibit great detail in south and central Utah. Powell's surveying is also used in Dutton's <u>Atlas to Accompany the Monograph on the Tertiary History of the Grand Cañon District</u>.

All these surveys were combined in 1879 to form the United States Geological Survey. Many of their projects and maps were left unfinished, though their publications kept appearing until 1889. A final map associated with this year is Edward Freyhold's second revision in 1879 of Lt. G. K. Warren's great map of 1857 with the blank spaces of the 1868 revision filled in with information from the surveys of the 1870's.

Commercial and Other Federal Mapping, 1879-1900

During the 1870's, several new commercial atlas and map publishers appeared, including the firms of Asher & Adams, Ormando Willis Gray and Frank Gray, Gaylord Watson; and Rand McNally & Co., Samuel Augustus Mitchell, Joseph Hutchins Colton, Alvin Jewett Johnson, and Hubert Howe Bancroft continued to publish new editions of their maps and atlases. Beginning in 1876, the United States General Land Office began publishing large maps of the states and

territories where public lands were sold which have become well
known. Editions of their Utah map appeared in 1876, 1879, 1884,
1889, 1893, 1902, 1908, 1915, 1926, 1936, and 1943. These General
Land Office maps formed the basis for many commercial maps. A popular cartographic form of the 1870's was the "bird's-eye view",
a perspective drawing from an oblique angle at an altitude of 2,000
or 3,000 feet. Brigham City, Corrine, Logan, Ogden, Provo, and
Salt Lake City were mapped in this manner.

The United States Geological Survey assumed the major re-
sponsibility for mapping in the United States when it was organized
in 1879. Continuing with material supplied by the four great surveys of the West, it began issuing topographical maps of Utah covering one degree of latitude and longitude at the scale of 1:250,000.
Seventeen out of a possible twenty-three maps covering Utah at this
scale were issued between 1884 and 1896, with some slight subsequent revisions (figure 2).

Because of the work of Federal surveys, all of Utah west
of the Colorado River had been mapped reasonably well by 1880. The
last large blank on the map of Utah, the area between the Abajo
Mountains and Navajo Mountain in southeastern Utah, was filled in
by 1890.

Maps of these Federal surveys were constructed by triangulation and plane table surveys. The art of transmitting terrain
to a sheet of paper accurately was a tremendous challenge. First,
the topographers established a network of triangles from an established base line to prominent mountain peaks, such as from Mount

United States Geological Survey

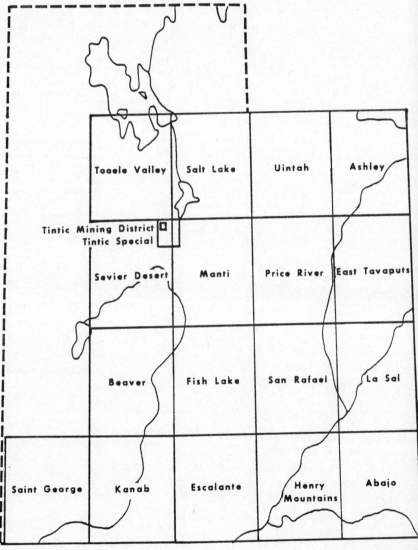

figure 2

Nebo to Wheeler Peak, to establish the exact positions of major

features. Next, a network of secondary triangulation of points

about six or eight miles apart was fixed. With these points math-

ematically determined, the topographers would sketch from the

mountain tops the drainage system and terrain they saw before them.

During the 1880's, the publishing houses of George Franklin

Cram and William H. Bradley began printing popular maps of Utah,

while the venerable firms of Samuel Augustus Mitchell, Alvin Jewett

Johnson, and Joseph Hutchins Colton left the map publishing busi-

ness. The most important Utah map of the 1880's is Joseph O. West's

New Sectional & Topographic Map of Utah published by authority of

the Territorial Assembly in 1885. Much like Froiseth's maps, it

is the most detailed map of the decade.

In 1867, the D. A. Sanborn National Insurance Diagram Bu-

reau began making very large scale (usually fifty feet to an inch)

maps of American cities and towns to determine for fire insurance

underwriters the potential fire hazards. These maps color coded

individual buildings by type of construction and gave very detail-

ed information on other features relevant to fire hazards such as

firewalls, chimneys, windows, doors, partitions, and fire hydrants.

Of the seventy-two Utah communities known to have been mapped by

the Sanborn Company, twenty-two had been surveyed before 1900.

The earliest ones known, Brigham City, Corrine, Ogden, and Salt

Lake City, were mapped in 1884. The earlier editions of these maps

often included only the commercial and industrial districts, but

by 1890 usually included residential neighborhoods as well.

By 1890, the major features of the Utah landscape had been mapped. The commercial cartographic houses, led by Rand McNally, continued to chronicle the advance of civilization across the face of Utah. The last decade of the century saw an increase of thematic maps or topical mapping. There were maps of real estate and land developments, maps of mining claims, forest reserves, water resources, soil surveys, and postal routes.

In 1896, Utah finally became a State of the Union. The new State Legislature commissioned B. A. M. Froiseth to make a larger and more detailed version of his monumental map of Utah. Published in 1898, it is 65 by 49 inches at the scale of 1:380,160 or six miles to an inch. It accurately shows Utah at the close of the nineteenth century as a rugged, though settled, land, well connected by roads and railroads. It is a far different scene than that depicted by Alexander von Humboldt at the beginning of the century.

Chapter II
1777 - 1849

1. <u>1778</u>

Plano Geographico de la tierra descubierta, nuebamente, a los Rumbos Norte Noroeste, y Oest del Nuebo Mexico. demarcada por mi Don Bernardo de Miera Pacheco que entró á hacer su descubrimiento, en compañia de los RR.s PP.s Fr. Francisco Atanasio Doming.s y Fr. Silbestre Veles, segun consta en el Diario y Derrotero que se hizo y se remitio á S. M. por mano de su Virrei con otro Plano a la letra: el que, dedica Al Sr. D.n Theadoro de la Crois, del Insigne Orden Teutonica Comandante General en Gefe de Linea y Provincias de esta America Septentrional, por su mag. Heco en Sn Phe. el Real de Chiguagua. Año de 1778.

72 x 84 cm. colored, ca 1:1,200,000.

The Rio de S. Buenaventura (Green River) flows into the Lacuna Miera (Sevier Lake); Utah Lake and the Great Salt Lake (Laguna de los Timpanogos) are one body of water with a narrow strait separating the two lakes with an outlet to the west indicated. Each day's camping places are noted. This issue is Wheat's "Type C."

Another issue found is <u>Plano Geografico de los Descu-brimientos hechos por. Sr. Bernardo Miera y Pacheco y los RR.s PP.s</u>

Fr. Francisco Atanasio Domingues y Fr. Silvestre Veles. S. Felipe
Rt. de Chiguagua Año de 1778. "A facsimile of the original in
the Western American Collection of the Beinecke Rare Book and
Manuscript Library, Yale University, New Haven, Connecticut. Repro-
duced by the Meriden Gravure Company 1970." This issue is a Wheat
"Type A."

Miera maps of the Dominauez-Escalante expedition are grouped
by Carl I. Wheat as follows by the type of ornamentation rather than
content which is similar:

Type A is undecorated and dedicated to the Viceroy.

Type B is decorated with a tree and serpent and dedicated
to the Caballero Croix.

Type C is decorated by bearded Indians and a papal chariot.

Wheat 173, 174, 176, 177, 178, 179; Lowery 593.

BYU, UU, UHS.

2. 1804

Carte Generale du Royaume de la Nouvelle Espagne depuis
le parallele de 16° jusqu'au parallele de 38° (latitude nord)
Dressée sur les observations astronomiques et sur l'ensemble des
materiaux qui existoient a Mexico, au commencement de l'annee
1804. Par Alexandre de Humboldt. L. Aubert pere scripsit. Dessiné
á Mexico par l'auteur en 1804., perfectionné par le même, par M. M.
Friesen, Oltmans et Thuilier 1809. Graré par Barriere et l'ecriture
par L. Aubert pere, á Paris.

69 x 100 cm.

Utah information is from Miera. This is the best known
source for Utah geography until the 1830's. Published in <u>Atlas</u>
<u>Geographique et Physique du Royaume de la Nouvelle Espagne</u> . . .
Paris, 1811.

Phillips 2682; Wheat 272.

LC.

3. <u>1827</u>

Partie du Mexique. Amér. Sep. N: 47.

43 x 55 cm., ca 1:1,500,000.

Shows the area from 36° to 42° North and from 110° to 116°
West. Utah information is from Miera including Lac de Timpanogos
(Great Salt Lake), Sierra de Timpanogos (Uintah Mountains), and
Rio de Sn. Buenaventura (Green River) flowing WSW into Teguayo
Lac Sale (Sevier Lake). The route of the Dominguez-Escalante
expedition shown. Includes note supposing northern Utah to be the
ancestral homeland of the Aztecs.

Credited by Tejas Galleries 15-315 to Vandermaalen,
Brussels, 1827.

Wheat 378; Phillips 749.

BYU.

4. <u>1834</u>

Nouvelle carte du Mexique et d'une partie des provinces
unies de l'Amerique Centrale. Dedie a l'Acadamie Royale des Sciences
de l'Institute de France. Par A. H. Brué, Geographe du Roi, de la
commission centrale de la Societé de Geographie de Paris, membre
honoaire de celle de Londres & a Paris. 1834. Chez Me. Ve. Brué,

rue des Macons-Sorbonne, No. 11, et chez les principaux marchands
de cartes geographiques. Oeuvre posthume.

93 x 63 cm.

This map and his 1833 map of North America (Wheat 401,
Phillips p888) are the first printed maps to incorporate Jedediah
Smith's explorations indicating a basin with no outlet to the sea.
The 1833 map shows places mentioned by Smith; this 1834 map also
shows Smith's trail. Many notes in French.

Wheat 404.

LC.

5. 1837

A map of the sources of the Colorado and Big Salt Lake,
Platte, Yellow-Stone, Muscle-Shell, Missouri, and Salmon and Snake
Rivers, branches of the Columbia River. Engr. by S. Stiles. New
York.

39 x 42 cm.

The Great Salt Lake, called "Lake Bonneville"; "Bear River,"
and "Weber's River," are named. Bear Lake is "Lit. Snake Lake."
Information for Utah based on the explorations of Joseph Reddeford
Walker in 1833.

Published in The Rocky Mountains . . . from the journal of
Captain B. L. E. Bonneville . . . by Washington Irving, Philadelphia,
Carey, Lea & Blanchard, 1837.

Wheat 423

LC.

6. <u>1837</u>

Map of the Territory West of the Rocky Mountains. Engr.
by S. Stiles.

41 x 43 cm.

"Lake Bonneville" (Great Salt Lake) is oval with four
islands. A small "Eutaw Lake," not on the other Bonneville map, is
a few miles to the east and drains into Lake Bonneville. Ashley's
Lake and a Lost River and an unnamed lake are 70 and 210 miles south
respectively of Lake Bonneville.

Published in The Rocky Mountains . . . from the journals
of Captain B. L. E. Bonneville . . . by Washington Irving, Philadelphia, Carey, Lea & Blanchard, 1837.

Wheat 424.

UHS, BYU.

7. <u>1838</u>

Map of the United States Territory of Oregon West of the
Rocky Mountains. Exhibiting the various Trading Posts or Forts
occupied by the British Hudson Bay Company: connected with the
Western and Northwestern Fur Trade. Compiled in the Bureau of
Topographical Engineers, from the latest authorities, under the
direction of Col. J. J. Abert, by Wash: Hood. 1838. M. H.
Stansbury dele.

48 x 53 cm.

"Youta or Great Salt Lake or Lake Bonneville" is rectangular
with no islands. Bear River is called "White Mud R." Hood tried
to revive the myth of the Buenaventura R. draining the interior.

Another issue has "W. J. Stone Sc. Washn." A note on the northern boundary of the U.S. in the lower left.

Published in Senate Bill 206, 25th Congress, 2nd Session and in House Document 101 and Senate Document 470, 25th Congress, 2nd Session. Serial 318 and 325.

Wheat 433.

GSL, SLP, LC, UU.

8. <u>1839</u>

Map of the United States of North America with Parts of the adjacent countries, by David H. Burr. (Late Topographer to the Post Office) Geographer to the House of Representatives of the U.S. Entered . . . 1839 by David H. Burr.

92 x 125 cm.

The outline of the Great Salt Lake is much improved over Bonneville and Hood, including five islands. "Utaw Lake" is moved a small distance south to a position five miles southeast of the Great Salt Lake. "Ashley's Lake" (Sevier Lake) and Lost River (Bear River) and Lost Lake are to the south. Virgin River is called "Adams River." Burr shows the Great Basin according to Jedidiah Smith's geography and marks his routes.

Wheat 441.

LC, UU, BYU, UHS.

9. <u>1841</u>

Map of the Oregon Territory by the U. S. Ex. Ex. Charles Wilkes Esqr. Commander. 1841. J. H. Young & Sherman & Smith, N.Y.

59 x 87 cm.

Wilkes shows only the northern third of Utah and includes information from Fremont's 1842 expedition. Utah Lake is part of "Youta Lake" (Great Salt Lake) and is separated by a narrow strait. Weber River is "New R." Bear Lake is "Little Lake."

Printed in Narrative of the United States Exploring Expedition during the years 1838, 1839, 1840, 1841, 1842 . . . Philadelphia, Lea & Blanchard, 1845.

Wheat 457.

GSL, LDSH, UU, LC.

10. 1841

Map of Upper California by the U.S. Ex. Ex. and best authorities. 1841.

22 x 29 cm.

Utah west of the "Colorado Range" (Wasatch Range) is labeled "Great Sandy Plain." The Colorado River flows south from the Wind River Range closely paralleling the "Colorado Range." Three unnamed lakes are south of "Youta Lake" in Utah.

Published in The Narrative of the United States Exploring Expedition during the years 1838, 1839, 1840, 1841, 1842 . . . Philadelphia, Lea & Blanchard, 1845.

Wheat 458.

LC.

11. 1844

Carte de la Côte de l'Amérique sur l'Océan Pacifique Septentrional comprenant le Territoire de l'Orégon, les Californies,

la Mer Vermeille, Partie des Territoires de la Compagnie de la
Baie d'Hudson, et de l'Amérique Russe. Dressée par Mr. Duflot de
Mofras. Attaché á la Légation de France á Mexico; Pour servir á
l'intelligence de son Voyage d'exploration Publié par Ordre du
Roi, sous les Auspices de Mr. Le Maréchal Duc de Dalmatie, President
de conseil des ministres et de Mr. Le Ministre des Affairs Étrangéres.
Paris. 1844. Le plan gravé par Jacobs. L'écriture gravée par
Hacq.

      91 x 57 cm. colored, 1:5,555,555.

      "Lac salé Youta ou Timpanogos" is basically square with a
small unnamed Utah Lake draining in from the southeast. There is a
larger unnamed lake positioned 100 miles SSW of the Great Salt Lake.
There are nineteen Indian villages named along Escalante's route in
southern Utah. Village of "Sn. Bernardo" is halfway between Utah
Lake and the Great Salt Lake. "Depot de la Compie Amerne des
Fourrurs" is halfway up the eastern shore of the Great Salt Lake.
The routes of Dominguez-Escalante, Spanish Trail, Oregon Trail,
"Le Cape Smith," and other fur traders are marked.

      Published in Exploration der Terretoire de l'Oregon, des
Californies et de la Mer Vermeille, éxecutée pendant les années
1840, 1841 et 1842, par M. Duflot de Mofras, Attaché a la Légation
de France a Mexico. Ouvrage Publié par Ordre du Roi, Sous les
Auspices de M. Le Maréchal Soult, Duc de Dalmatie, President du
Conseil et de M. Le Ministre des Affaires Étrangérs. Atlas.
Paris, Arthus Bertrand Editeur, Libraire de la Society de Geographie,
Rue Haute. Feuille No. 23. 1844.

Wheat 474; Phillipa 1457; Phillips p897.

BYU, BL, LC.

12. <u>1845</u>

Map of an exploring expedition to the Rocky Mountains in the
year 1842 and to Oregon and North California in the years 1843-44
by Brevet Capt. J. C. Fremont of the Corps of Topographical Engineers
under the orders of Col. J. J. Abert, Chief of the Topographical
Bureau. Lith. by E. Weber & Co., Baltimore Md.

77 x 129 cm., 1:3,000,000.

Along the top is a "Profile of the route from the mouth of
the Kansas to the Pacific by Capt. J. C. Fremont in 1843." Displays
Fremont's routes and the features seen by him. A note running
through the empty Great Basin reads, "The Great Basin: diameter 11°
of latitude, 10° of longitude: elevation above the sea between 4
and 5000 feet: surrounded by lofty mountains: contents almost
unknown, but believed to be filled with rivers and lakes which have
no communication with the sea, deserts and oases which have never
been explored, and savage tribes, which no traveller has seen or
described. See Fremont's Report, pages 275-6."

Published in <u>Report of the Exploring Expedition to the</u>
<u>Rocky Mountains in the year 1842 and to Oregon and North California</u>
<u>in the years 1843-44 . . . .</u> Washington, Gales and Seaton, 1845.
28th Congress, 2nd Session, Senate Executive Document 174 and House
Executive Document 166, Serial 461 and 467. Superintendent of
Documents #W7.5:F88.

Wheat 497; Phillips p895.

LDSH, BYU, UHS, BL, UU, USU, WCL, LC.

13. <u>1845</u>

Map of the Eastern and Middle portions of North America to illustrate the history of California, Oregon and other countries on the northwest coast of America by Robert Greenhow. Compiled from the best Authorities by Robert Greenhow. Drawn by George H. Ringgold. Engraved by E. F. Woodward. Philada.

57 x 65 cm., ca 1:8,870,000.

"Utah Salt Lake" is rectangular with the Bear River flowing north seventy miles, then west seventy miles to enter at the northeast corner. Sevier Lake is called "Ashleys Lake," and Utah Lake is small and unnamed. There are two unnamed lakes in southwest Utah west of a possible Virgin River. An empty Great Basin is labeled "Sand Plains Containing Salt Lakes & Swamps." Greenhow's geography is taken from Wilkes and Fremont.

Another issue published in <u>The Claim of the United States to Oregon . . .</u> London, Wiley & Putnam. Day & Hagbe Lithrs. to the Queen, 1846.

Wheat 512.

UU, BYU.

14. <u>1846</u>

A New Map of Texas Oregon and California with the regions adjoining compiled from the most recent authorities. Philadelphia. Published by S. Augustus Mitchell. N. E. Corner of Market and Seventh Streets, 1846. Entered . . . 1846 by H. N. Burroughs.

54 x 50 cm. colored, 1:6,650,000.

Utah information is based on Fremont. The Oregon Trail and Fremont's route shown through Utah. The Texas panhandle extends into Wyoming to 42° N. Utah is included in "Upper or New California" which extends below the Gila River on a line from Puerto Peñasco to above Tucson, then to a point northeast of Lago Guzman. There is a narrow strip of unclaimed land along the west bank of the Rio Grande from El Paso to its headwaters between Texas and Upper or New California. Oregon extends north to 54°40' N. Note in northern Nevada: "From the Great Salt Lake westward there is a succession of Rivers and Lakes which have no outlet to the sea, nor any connection with the Columbia river, nor with the Colorado river of the Gulf of California." Note in southern Nevada: "The unexplored region enclosed on the W. by the Sierra Nevada and on the east by the Bear R. and Wahsatch Mts. has been called the GREAT INTERIOR BASIN OF CALIFORNIA, its circuit is about 1800 miles, some portions of its surface are arid and sandy and destitute of water and grass, while in other quarters, rivers and lakes are known to abound." In the lower left is a mileage chart "Emigrant Route from Missouri to Oregon" with distances between twenty-four points between Westport and Oregon City by interval and cumulative. This map was used by Brigham Young on his trek westward.

Wheat 520; Phillips p184.

LDSH, UHS, USU, UU, BYU, LC.

15. <u>1847</u>

    Mapa de los Estados Unidos de México, segun lo organizado y definido por las varias actos del Congreso de dicha Republica: y construido pos las mejores autoridades. Lo Publican J. Disturnell, 102 Broadway, Neuva York, 1847.

    74 x 104 cm. colored, 1:4,300,000.

    Mexico is colored by states; Alta California extends to 42° N. Utah geography is based on Fremont and his routes are shown, also the Spanish Trail. Texas claims all of New Mexico east of the Rio Grande.

    Phillips p410.

    LC, BYU.

16. <u>1847</u>

    Western Territories of the United States. Drawn & Eng. by Sherman & Smith. Entered . . . 1847 by D. F. Robinson . . .

    27 x 44 cm. colored, ca. 1:5,850,000.

    Colored by territories. Utah information based on Fremont. Copyright date of 1847 means it is the first map to show a "Great Salt Lake City (Mormon Set.)." Utah boundaries are from about 1850. There are fifteen settlements in the Sacramento-San Francisco area; none of them mining camps.

    UU.

17. <u>1848</u>

    Map of Oregon and Upper California from the Surveys of John Charles Fremont and other authorities. Drawn by Charles Preuss

Under the Order of the Senate of the United States, Washington City,
1848. Lith. by E. Weber & Co. Balto.

    85 x 67 cm., 1:3,000,000.

    Treaty lines of 1848 are shown in blue. Fremont's routes are
indicated. Fremont corrects the relationship of Utah Lake and Great
Salt Lake from his 1845 map. A "Mormon Fort" is shown at the top of
Utah Lake and "Mormon Settlements" indicated in Davis and Salt Lake
counties. Here the term "Great Basin" is first used and is surrounded by a solid ring of mountains. Sevier Lake and Sevier River
called Nicolette Lake and Nicolette River.

    Published in <u>Geographical Memoir upon Upper California in</u>
<u>Illustration of His Map of Oregon and California by John Charles</u>
<u>Fremont. Addressed to the Senate of the United States</u>. Washington.
Wendell and Van Benthuysen, Printers, 1848. 30th Cong. 1st.
Sess. Sen. Misc. Doc. 148. Serial 511. Superintendent of Documents
#Y1.3:C12.

    Wheat 559; Phillips p184.

    WCL, GSL, UHS, USU, UU, BYU, LC.

18. <u>1849</u>

    Map of California, New Mexico and adjacent countries showing
the Gold Regions & c. New York. Published by J. Disturnell. 1849.
Printed at Ackermans rooms, 120 Fulton St.

    74 x 104 cm. colored, 1:4,300,000.

    Inset of "Routes from Vera Cruz and Alvarado to Mexico"
and two profiles. Utah geography is based on Fremont's 1845 map.
"Mormon ft" is on the channel from Utah Lake to Great Salt Lake.

There are notes from Fremont on the Great Salt Lake and Bear River Valley printed southwest of the lake.

BYU, USU (1859 imprint).

19. <u>1849</u>

Map of California, Oregon, Texas and the territories adjoining with routes & c. Published by J. H. Colton, No. 86 Cedar St., New York, 1849. Ackermans lith. 120 Fulton St., N.Y. Entered . . . 1849 by J. H. Colton . . .

48 x 42 cm. colored, ca. 1:6,300,000.

Shows United States west of 95° W. Utah information is from Fremont including the channel linking Utah Lake and Great Salt Lake. Fremont's routes are marked. A "Mormon Fort" is located near the northern end of the Utah Lake embayment. This edition omits Fremont's notes from the 1846 edition. Utah is part of "Upper or New California" with the southern boundary colored along the Gila River.

Another issue is published in <u>Oregon and California in 1848</u> by J. Quinn Thornton, D. Appleton & Co. New York, 1849.

Wheat 593.

LDSH, UHS.

20. <u>1849</u>

Map of the Emigrant Road from Independence Mo. to St. Francisco California by T. H. Jefferson. Part III.

30 x 38 cm.

Part three of a map in four parts similar to Charles Preuss' 1846 map of the Oregon Trail in seven parts. Jefferson's route is

over the Hastings Cutoff south of Salt Lake. The emigrant road
comes down Weber Canyon. No sign of any settlements. The Jordan
River is called "Utah River." Many wells are shown in Tooele and
Skull Valleys.

Published with Accompaniement to the Map of the Emigrant Road
from Independence Mo. to St. Francisco California. New York, 1849.

Phillips p900.

LDSH, UU, UHS, BYU, LC.

21. 1849

A New Map of Texas Oregon and California with the Regions
Adjoining Compiled from the most recent authorities. Philadelphia.
Published by Thomas, Cowperthwait & Co. Market St. No 253. 1849.
Entered . . . 1845 by H. N. Burroughs.

53 x 49 cm. colored, 1:6,650,000.

Same basic map as the 1846 edition by Mitchell. Colored
by states and territories, ignoring the 1846 boundary lines in the
case of Texas, New Mexico, and Mexico. The California gold region is
colored separately. The colored U.S./Mexico boundary follows the
treaty line of 1848 along the Gila River, while the printed
boundary follows the 1846 edition. New Mexico is colored to include
only the Rio Grande drainage above "Paso del Norte." Trails are
drawn in red. "Salt Lake City (Mormon Set.)" is shown on the
shores of Great Salt Lake.

Bound with seventy-six page booklet Description of Oregon
and California Embracing an Account of the Gold Regions to Which is
Added an Appendix Containing Descriptions of Various Kinds of Gold,

and Methods of Testing its Genuineness. With a Large and Accurate

Map of Oregon and California Compiled from the Latest Authorities.

A different issue of Wheat 629.

BYU.

Chapter III
1850 - 1859

22. <u>1850</u>

Map of the State of California, the Territories of Oregon
& Utah and the chief part of New Mexico. Entered . . . 1845 by
H. N. Burroughs . . .

38 x 31 cm. colored, 1:6,700,000.

Utah geography is from Fremont's 1845 map including the
channel between Utah Lake and Great Salt Lake. Salt Lake City is
the only settlement shown. The Oregon Trail, Spanish Trail, and
Fremont's routes are shown. The Great Basin is called "Fremont
Basin." "Tueson" is shown fifty miles east northeast of Tubac.

A <u>New Universal Atlas</u> . . . Philadelphia, Thomas, Cowperthwait, 1851. Entered . . . 1850 by Thomas, Cowperthwait, p. 37.

Phillips 805 (under S. A. Mitchell).

LDSH, LC.

23. <u>1850</u>

Map of the United States and their Territories between the
Mississippi and the Pacific Ocean and of part of Mexico. Compiled
in the Bureau of the Corps of Topogl. Engs. under a Resolution of
the U. S. Senate. From the best authorities which could be obtained.
1850. Engraved by Sherman and Smith. New-York.

98 x 106 cm., 1:3,168,000, or 50 miles to 1 inch.

Utah geography is based on Fremont. Relief is by hachures. "G.S.L. City" is the only settlement in Utah. A more accurate shape of the Great Salt Lake indicates information from Stansbury's surveys. This is a synthesis of all previous U.S. Topographical Engineers' explorations and maps and is the best and most accurate to date.

Phillips p900.

LDSH, LC.

24. <u>1850</u>

A New Map of the State of California, the Territories of Oregon and Utah, and the chief portion of New Mexico. Entered . . . 1850 by Thomas, Cowperthwait & Co.

38 x 30 cm. colored, 1:6,700,000.

California and New Mexico are colored by counties; there are no counties shown in Utah. Shows roads in California. Shows Fremont's Trail, the Oregon Trail, and the Spanish Trail through the Great Basin, here named "Fremont Basin." The shoreline of the Great Salt Lake is from Fremont's 1845 map. There are three towns in Utah, "Salt Lake City (Mormon Set.)," Ogden which is called "Brownsville," and a "Blooming Grove" in between.

A <u>New Universal Atlas</u> . . . Philadelphia, S. Augustus Mitchell, 1850, p. 37. Another issue is "Entered . . . 1851 by Thomas, Cowperthwait & Co." and is page 37 in Mitchell's <u>New Atlas of North and South America</u>. Philadelphia, Thomas, Cowperthwait & Co. 1851.

Another issue is page 37 of <u>A New Universal Atlas</u> . . . Philadelphia,
S. Augustus Mitchell, 1852.

Phillips 807; Wheat 725, 756.

UHS, BYU, LC.

25. <u>1850</u>

Map of a Reconnaissance between Fort Leavenworth on the
Missouri River and the Great Salt Lake in the Territory of Utah,
made in 1849 and 1850 under the orders of Col. J. J. Abert, Chief
of the Topographical Bureau, by Capt. Howard Stansbury of the Corps
of Topographical Engineers, aided by Lieut. J. W. Gunnison, Corps of
Topographical Engineers, and Albert Carrington. The Adjacent
country laid down from the latest and most authentic data. Drawn by
Lieut. Gunnison and Charles Preuss. Ackerman Lith. 379 Broadway,
N.Y.

73 x 173 cm., 1:1,000,000.

Utah is shown west to Pilot Peak and south past Nephi.
Shows roads and trails. There is a large Great Salt Lake City, but
no other settlements except for an unnamed one on a City Creek near
Levan.

This map accompanies <u>Exploration and Survey of the Valley</u>
<u>of the Great Salt Lake of Utah, Including a Reconnaissance of a</u>
<u>New Route Through the Rocky Mountains</u>. 32nd Congress Special
Session Senate Executive Document, 3 March 1851, Serial 608,
Superintendent of Documents #W7.5:St2, and <u>An Expedition to the Valley</u>
<u>of the Great Salt Lake of Utah</u> by Howard Stansbury, U.S. Engineer
Dept. Philadelphia, Lippincott & Grambo & Co., 1852.

Wheat 764; Phillips p947.

UU, BL, LC, LDSH, UHS, BYU.

26. <u>1850</u>

Map of the Great Salt Lake and adjacent country in the Territory of Utah. Surveyed in 1849 and 1850, under the orders of Col. J. J. Abert, Chief of the Topographical Bureau, by Capt. Howard Stansbury of the Corps of Topographical Engineers, aided by Lieut. J. W. Gunnison Corps of Topographical Engineers and Albert Carrington. Drawn by Lieut. Gunnison and Charles Preuss. Ackerman Lith. 319 Broadway N.Y.

110 x 76 cm., 1:240,000.

The first detailed map of Utah extending from Cache Valley to Yoab (sic) Valley. Great topographical detail of the Wasatch front and the Great Salt Lake including soundings in the Great Salt Lake and Utah Lake in feet, also settlements and roads. This is the first accurate survey of the lake.

It accompanies the same documents listed in the previous entry.

Wheat 765.

SLP, BL, LDSH, UHS, BYU, LC.

27. <u>1851</u>

Map of the Territory of New Mexico compiled by Bvt. 2nd Lt. Jno. G. Parke, U.S.T.E. assisted by Mr. Richard H. Kern by order of Bvt. Col. Jno. Munroe, U.S.A. Comdg. 9th Mil. Dept. Drawn by R. H. Kern. Santa Fe, N.M. 1851. Constructed under general orders from Col. J. J. Abert, Chief Corps of Topogl. Engrs. Lith. of J. & D. Major 177 Broadway, N.Y.

62 x 85 cm., 1:2,280,000.

Shows southern Utah up to 39° N. A list of sources is in the lower right. Utah's geography is from Fremont.

Phillips p494.

LC, UU, USU, BYU.

28. 1852

A new map of the State of California, the Territories of Oregon & Utah. Compiled after the best authorities. 1852. Hildburghausen. Published by the Bibliographic Institution. E. Biedermann sculp.

38 x 31 cm., ca. 1:6,450,000.

Shows the Spanish Trail, Oregon Trail, Fremont's routes and other roads in California. Inset of "San Francisco and Environs" in the lower left.

Meyer's Hand-Atlas. No. 44.

UU.

29. 1853

A New Map of the State of California, the Territories of Oregon, Washington, Utah & New Mexico. Published by Thomas, Cowperthwait & Co. No. 253. Market St. Philadelphia. Entered . . . 1853 by Thomas, Cowperthwait.

37 x 29 cm. colored, 1:6,650,000.

Colored by counties. Fillmore City is the capitol of Utah Territory. The town of Brownsville is ten miles west of the town of

Ogden, and Tueson (sic) is fifty miles east northeast of Tubac. The

Great Basin is called "Fremont Basin." Shows roads, explorers'

routes, and the Oregon Trail. Shows Gadsden Treaty line of 1854.

A New Universal Atlas . . . Philadelphia, Thomas, Cowper-

thwait & Co. 1853, p. 37. Another issue "Entered and published by

Charles Desilver, No. 253 Market Street, Philadelphia . . . 1850

by Thomas, Cowperthwait & Co."

Phillips 809; Wheat 813.

LDSH, UU, LC.

30. 1853

New Map of California, Oregon, Washington, Utah, and New

Mexico. Compiled from the latest authorities & surveys and engraved

by G. Schroeter. Published by J. Disturnell. New York, 1853.

60 x 67 cm, colored.

This and the previous Mitchell map are the first to show

counties in Utah including Desert County west of the Great Salt

Lake between Weber and Tooele Counties. Shows the old Spanish

Trail, Oregon Trail, Fremont's routes and nine towns in Utah.

Wheat 778; Phillips p947.

GSL, LC, BL, BYU.

31. 1854

General map showing the countries explored & surveyed by

the United States & Mexican boundary commission, in the years 1850,

51, 52, & 53, under the direction of John R. Bartlett, U. S.

Commissioner. J. H. Colton & Co. No. 174 William St. New York.

D. McLellan Print. 26 Spruce St.

39 x 49 cm.

Shows several Utah towns plus Fremont's 1844-45 route, the old Spanish Trail, and the emigrant road.

BL.

32. <u>1854</u>

Map to illustrate Capt. Bonneville's Adventures among the Rocky Mountains. Compiled by J. H. Colton. No. 86 Cedar Street. New York. Geo. P. Putnam. 1854.

29 x 45 cm., ca. 1:6,100,000.

Many differences from Bonneville's own map. This is a current Colton map with Bonneville's routes overprinted.

UHS.

33. <u>1855</u>

California, Utah, Lr. California and New Mexico. Drawn and engraved by T. Ettling. Day & Son, Lithrs. to the Queen.

41 x 31 cm.

Published in the <u>Weekly Dispatch Atlas</u>, London.

BL.

34. <u>1855</u>

Explorations and Surveys for a Rail Road from the Mississippi River to the Pacific Ocean. War Department. Route near the 41st Parallel. Map No. 1. From the Valley of the Green River to the Great Salt Lake; from Explorations and Surveys made under the direction of the Hon. Jefferson Davis, Secretary of War. by Capt. E. G. Beckwith, 3rd Artillery. F. W. Egloffstein, Topographer for the

Route. 1855. Selmar Sieberts Engraving and Printing Establishment, Washington, D.C.

52 x 46 cm. "Scale of 12 miles to 1 inch or 1:760,320."

Proposed route splits at Henefer: one goes down the Weber River, the other through Kamas and Provo Canyon to rejoin at Black Rock west of Salt Lake. American Fork is called "Lake City."

Published in Reports of Explorations and Surveys to Ascertain the Most Practicable and Economical Route for a Railroad from the Mississippi River to the Pacific Ocean. Made Under the Direction of the Secretary of War in 1853-6. Volume XI. Washington, Beverly Tucker, Printer, 1855. Senate Ex. Doc. No. 78, 33d Congress, 2nd Session and House Ex. Doc. No. 91. Serial 768 and 801. Superintendent of Documents #W7.14:11.

Wheat 822.

UHS, BYU, LC.

35. 1855

Explorations and Surveys for a Rail Road Route from the Mississippi River to the Pacific Ocean. War Department. Route Near the 41st Parallel. Map No. 2. From Great Salt Lake to the Humboldt Mountains; from Explorations and Surveys made under the direction of the Hon. Jefferson Davis Secretary of War by Capt. E. G. Beckwith 3d Artillery. F. W. Egloffstein Topographer for the Route. 1855. Selmar Siebert's Engraving and Printing Establishment. Washington, D.C.

53 x 46 cm. "Scale of 12 miles to 1 inch or 1:760,320.

Two proposed routes cross the southern edge of the Great Salt Lake Desert and rejoin south of Pilot Peak.

Printed in the same documents as the previous map.

Wheat 823.

UU, USU, BYU, LC.

36. <u>1855</u>

Explorations and Surveys for a Rail Road Route from the
Mississippi River to the Pacific Ocean. War Department Route Near
the 38th and 39th Parallels. Map No. 4. From the Coo-Che-To-Pa
Pass to the Wahsatch Mountains from Explorations and Surveys made
under the direction of the Hon. Jefferson Davis Secretary of War
by Capt. J. W. Gunnison. Topl. Engrs. assisted by Capt. E. G.
Beckwith 3d Artillery. R. H. Kern, Topographer in the field.
Map made under the supervision of Capt. E. G. Beckwith 3d Artillery
by F. W. Egloffstein, Topographer for the Route. 1855. Engr. by
Selmar Siebert.

80 x 59 cm. "Scale of 12 miles to 1 inch or 1:760,320."

Captain Gunnison and Richard Kern were killed on this survey
near the site of Delta and the map finished by Beckwith and
Egloffstein. Gunnison's route follows the Gunnison and Grand Rivers
to Moab, the Spanish Trail to the Green River, and west to the
Sevier Valley and Wasatch Mountains.

Published in what is popularly called the <u>Pacific Railroad
Reports</u>, vol. 11, which is the same set as the three previous maps
appeared in.

Wheat 846.

USU, BYU, LC.

37. <u>1855</u>

Skeleton map exhibiting the route explored by Capt. J. W. Gunnison U.S.A. 38 Parallel of Latitude. (1853). Also that of the 41 Parallel of Latitude explored by Lieutenant E. G. Beskwith (sic) 3d Arty. (1854). Drawn by F. W. Egloffstein. Lith. of Sarony & Co. N.Y.

64 x 95 cm.

Preliminary map showing the routes of Gunnison and Beckwith with some topographical detail bordering their routes. Published in <u>Report of the Secretary of War on the several Pacific Railroad Explorations</u>. Washington, A. O. P. Nicholson Printer, 1855. 33rd Congress, 1st Session, House Doc. 129, Serial 739.

Wheat 842; Phillips p903.

LC.

38. <u>1855</u>

Map Showing the different routes travelled over by the Detachments of the overland Command in the Spring of 1855 from Salt Lake City to the Bay of San Francisco. Ackerman Lith. 379 Broadway, N.Y. Senate Ex. Doc. No. 1, 1st Session, 34th Congress.

56 x 46 cm., ca. 1:2,000,000.

Routes of Col. Steptoe shown in detail from "G.S. Lake City" to Los Angeles. "Mt. Meadows," and "Gunnison's Massacre" are located, and there is a "U.S. Camp" near the site of Stockton.

Published in <u>Report of Captin Rufus Ingalls of the March of Col. Steptoe from Fort Leavenworth to California</u>, Serial 843.

Wheat 868.

USU, UHS, LDSH, BYU, LC.

39. <u>1855</u>

Territories of New Mexico and Utah. Published by J. H.
Colton & Co. No. 172 William St. New York. Entered . . . 1855
by J. H. Colton & Co. . .

29 x 36 cm. colored, 1:4,435,000.

Colored by counties. Fillmore City is the capital. Shows
Fremont's routes, the Spanish Trail, and "route explored for Pacific
RR." Sevier Lake is called Nicolette Lake and is shown to be dry.
"Preuss Lake" is out on the Escalante Desert.

<u>Colton's Atlas of the World</u>. New York, J. H. Colton,
Baltimore, James Waters, 1856, p. 51. Entered . . . 1855 by J. H.
Colton.

Wheat 832; Phillips 10269.

LDSH, UU, SLP, BL, BYU, LC.

40. <u>1855</u>

Utah, and the Overland Routes to it, from the Missouri
River. Published with "Route from Liverpool to G.S.L. Valley" by
Franklin D. Richards: Liverpool. 1855.

29 x 47 cm., 1:6,969,600 or 110 miles to 1 inch.

Utah counties numbered with a list in the lower left. The
Mormon Pioneer Trail and Fremont's routes are marked.

Published in <u>Route from Liverpool to Great Salt Lake Valley</u>
. . . edited by James Linforth. Liverpool: published by Franklin
D. Richards, 36 Islington, London: Latter-Day Saints Book Depot,
35, Jewin Street, City MDCCCLV (Reproduced in Salt Lake City, 1858).

Another edition titled Route from Liverpool by Frederick Piercy,
London, 1855.

SCL, UHS, BYU.

41. 1856

Western States including California, Oregon, Utah, Washington,
New Mexico, Nebraska, Kansas, Indian Territory & c. Drawn & Engraved
by J. Bartholomew. Printed in colours by Schenk & McFarlane.

56 x 42 cm.

Black's Atlas of North America. Edinburgh. A. & C. Black,
1856, No. 18.

Phillips 1835; Phillips p906.

LC.

42. 1856

A New Map of the State of California, the Territories of
Oregon, Washington, Utah & New Mexico. Published by Charles
Desilver No. 251 Market Street Philadelphia. Entered . . . 1856
by Charles Desilver . . .

37 x 29 cm colored, ca. 1:6,650,000.

Colored by counties, shows roads, explorers' routes, and
proposed railroad routes. The Gadsden Purchase is labeled "Proposed
Arizona Territory."

A New Universal Atlas. Philadelphia, C. Desilver, 1856, p.
37.

Phillips 4336 (listed under S. Augustus Mitchell).

LDSH, UU, LC.

43. <u>1856</u>

United States: Sheet 1. Western States.

53 x 62 cm. colored, ca. 1:4,250,000.

A "Lake Ashley" is in the Escalante Desert and a very small unnamed Bear Lake north of the Utah border.

<u>Philip's Commercial Atlas of the World</u>. London, George Philip & Son, 1856, sheet 57.

LDSH, BYU.

44. <u>1856</u>

Map showing the Extent of Surveys in the Territory of Utah 1856. Examined and approved this 30th Sept. 1856. Sur. Genl. David H. Burr of Utah. P. S. Duval & Son Lith. Phila.

83 x 39 cm., 1:316,800 or 5 miles to 1 inch.

Shows the Wasatch Front from T.14N. to T.12S. and from R.7W. to R.3E. There are many different names on this map: Santaquin is "Summit Cr."; Pleasant Grove is "Battle Cr."; Alpine is "Mountain-ville"; Draper is "Willow Cr."; Brigham City is "Box Elder"; and North Ogden is "Ogden Hole."

Published as part of the 34th Cong. 3rd Sess. Senate Ex. Doc. No. 5. Serial 844.

Hargett 784.

USU, SLP, UHS, LDSH, UU, BYU, LC.

45. <u>1856</u>

Map of a Survey of the Indian Reservation on Spanish Fork Cr. Utah Territory--showing its connection with the U.S. Survey of the Territory: by David H. Burr; surveyor. Reserve established by Agent Hurt. April 1856.

43 x 55 cm., 1:40,000.

Shows the proposed Indian reservation extending from Spanish Fork Creek to West Mountain. "View of the Farmhouse, Indian Farm, Spanish Fork, U.T." is in the upper left corner and a "View of a section of the Irrigating Canal, Indian Farm, Spanish Fork U.T." is in the upper right corner.

BYU.

46. 1856

California. New York, D. Appleton & Co. 1856.

35 x 29 cm., ca. 1:3,000,000.

Inset of Utah and part of New Mexico.

Morse's General Atlas of the World. New York, D. Appleton & Co., 1856, p. 37.

Phillips 817 (listed under Charles W. Morse).

BL, LC.

47. 1857

Map of the United States and their territories between the Mississippi and the Pacific Ocean and part of Mexico compiled from Surveys made under the order of W. H. Emory, Major 1st Cavalry, U.S. Commissioner. And from the maps of the Pacific Railroad, General Land Office, and the Coast Survey. Projected and drawn under the supervision of Lt. N. Michler, Topl. Engrs. By Thomas Jeckyll, C. E. 1857-8. United States & Mexican Boundary Survey. General

Map. Selmar Siebert's Engraving and Printing Establishment.
Washington, D.C.

52 x 58 cm., "Scale 1:6,000,000."

Great topographic detail in the northern two-thirds of
Utah. The southern one-third on each side of Fremont's route is
labeled "Unexplored Territory." Salt Lake City is the only settlement
shown.

Published in Report of the United States and Mexican Boundary
Survey . . . Washington, Cornelius Wendell, 1857. Serial 862.

Phillips p907.

BYU, LC.

48. 1857

Map illustrating the general geological features of the
country west of the Mississippi River. Compiled from the Surveys
of W. H. Emory and from the Pacific Railroad Survey & other sources
by Professor James Hall, assisted by J. P. Lesley, Esq. Drawn by
Ths. Jeckyll, Lith. of Sarony, Major & Knapp. 499 Broadway, New
York.

50 x 59 cm. colored, 1:6,000,000.

Geologic features are colored on Emory's base map.

Published in Report of the United States and Mexican
Boundary Survey . . . Washington, Cornelius Wendell, 1857. Serial 862.

LC.

49. 1857

Map of the Territory of the United States from the Mississippi
to the Pacific Ocean. Ordered by the Hon. Jerr'n Davis, Secretary

of War. To accompany the Reports of the Explorations for a
Railroad Route. Made in accordance with the 10th and 11th sections of
the Army Appropriation Act of March 3rd 1853. Compiled from authorized explorations and other reliable data by Lieut. G. K. Warren.
Topl. Engrs. In the Office of Pacific R. R. Surveys, War Dep.
under the direction of Bvt. Maj. W. H. Emory. Topl. Engrs. in 1854
and of Capt. A. A. Humphreys. Topl. Engrs. 1854-5-6-7. Engr. by
Selmar Siebert.

      109 x 118 cm., 1:3,000,000.

      The best and most detailed map of its time. Topography
by E. Freyhold and L. W. Egloffstein. Drawn on the polyconic method.
Shows roads, trails, existing and proposed railroads. Camp Floyd
is shown in Utah.

      Published in <u>Reports of Explorations and Surveys, to</u>
<u>Ascertain the Most Practicable and Economical Route for a Railroad</u>
<u>from the Mississippi River to the Pacific Ocean. Made Under the</u>
<u>Direction of the Secretary of War, in 1853-6.</u> Volume XI.
Washington, Beverly Tucker Printer, 1855. 33rd Cong. 2nd Sess.
Senate Ex. Doc. No. 78. Serial 768 and 801. Superintendent of
Documents #W7.14:11.

      Wheat 936; Phillips p904.

      USU, LC, BYU, UU, LDSH.

50. <u>1857</u>

      Utah and New Mexico.

      13 x 15 cm. colored, ca. 1:4,750,000.

The information dates from 1854. Fillmore City is the capital and it is colored by counties. Made by the cerographic (wax) process.

Published in The Diamond Atlas by D. G. Colby. New York, S. N. Gaston, 1857.

Phillips 1180.

UHS, BYU, UU, LC.

51. 1858

The Dispatch Atlas. California, Utah, Lr. California, and New Mexico. Weekly Dispatch Atlas 139 Fleet Street. Day & Son, Lithrs. to the Queen. Drawn & Engraved by T. Ettling; 3, Red Lion Square. Holburn. Supplement to the Weekly Dispatch of Sunday January 31st 1858.

30 x 43 cm. colored.

Shows the Mormon route to San Bernardino and the Spanish Trail.

Wheat 942.

BL.

52. 1858

Sketch Exhibiting the Routes between Fort Laramie and the Great Salt Lake. From Explorations by J. C. Fremont, H. Stansbury. Capts. Corps of Topl. Engrs. E. G. Beckwith Lieut. 3 Art. T. F. Bryan Lieut. Topl. Engrs. And F. W. Lander Chf. Eng. Sth. Pss. Pacific Wagon Road. War Dept. Office of Explorations & Surveys. Drawn by E. Freyhold. Jary 1858. Lith. of Ritchie & Dunnavant,

Richmond Va. 2nd Edition Apr. 15, 1858. With corrections &
additions from Map prepared by Maj. F. J. Porter U.S.A.

50 x 80 cm., 1:1,000,000.

Shows roads and trails from south of Nephi to north of Ft.
Hall and east to Ft. Laramie.

First edition is Wheat 943; Phillips p907.

UU, UHS, LC.

53. <u>1858</u>

Map of Utah Territory showing the routes connecting it with
California and the East. Compiled in the Bureau of Topogr. Engrs.
of the War Departmt. from the latest and most reliable data 1858.
Lith. of Ritchie & Dunnavant Richmond Va.

79 x 108 cm., 1:1,500,000.

Shows roads and trails in an area bounded by Santa Fe, Ft.
Laramie, Sacramento, and Los Angeles. List of "Authorities"
including Fremont 1848; Stansbury/Gunnison 1849,50; Gunnison/Beckwith
1853,54. Nicolette River and Nicolette Lake now called Sevier
River and Sevier Lake. The only settlements shown are G. S. Lake
City, Provo, and Fillmore.

Wheat 960; Hargett 785; Phillips p947.

GSL, LC, BYU.

54. <u>1858</u>

Sketch of the Country between South Pass & the Great Salt
Lake. C. B. Graham, Lith. Washington, D.C. Sen. Ex. Doc. No. 11
and Ho. Ex. Doc. No. 2 1st Sess. 35th Cong.

44 x 55 cm., 1:1,000,000.

This map shows roads in the area from Levan to Ft. Hall and east to South Pass. The Provo River is called "Timpanogos R."; Provo is "Ft. Utah"; Nephi is "Nephie City." There is a small unnamed Bear Lake six miles long. Carl Wheat credits this map originally to Howard Stansbury in 1850.

Serial 922.

Wheat 958.

USU, UHS, BYU, LC.

55. 1858

Preliminary map of routes reconnoitred and opened in the Territory of Utah by Capt. J. H. Simpson, Corps of Topographical Engineers in the Fall of 1858 under the orders of Bvt. Brigadier General A. S. Johnston Commanding the Department of Utah. Lith. of Julius Bien, 60 Fulton Street, N.Y. 35th Cong. 2nd Sess. Senate Ex. Doc. No. 40.

76 x 112 cm., 1:316,000 or 5 miles to 1 inch.

Prominent features include the wagon roads through Utah from Fr. Bridger to Pilot Peak, the "Mormon Fortifications" in Echo Canyon and Emigration Canyon, and Capt. Beckwith's route in 1854. Shows temporary military camps in Reynold's Pass, southern Rush Valley, Tintic Valley, and two camps west of unnamed Nephi in "Youab Valley," one named "Camp Crossman."

Serial 984.

Wheat 998.

UU, UHS, BYU, LC.

56. <u>1858</u>

California, Oregon, Washington, Utah & New Mexico. Eng. by Geo. F. Sherman, N.Y., J. Wells, N.Y.

27 x 21 cm., ca. 1:9,500,000.

A curious map showing Brownsville and Ogden City thirty miles apart; Nephi City is in the San Pete Valley; Manti City is near the site of Emery; Fillmore City is in the Sevier Valley; and Parovan (sic) is twenty-five miles northwest of Cedar.

Published in <u>McNally's System of Geography</u>, Map No. 16 on page 40.

UHS, BYU.

57. <u>1859</u>

Map of Route of Father Escalante From Santa Fe to Lake Utah and back by way of Oraybe, Zuñi, & Acoma 1776-7. Explorations of Capt. J. H. Simpson, T. E. U. S. A. in 1859. Plate G.

22 x 24 cm., ca. 1:3,750,000.

Shows Escalante's route and Old Spanish Trail, where it differs, plus Simpson's routes in 1859, the Hastings Road, and the "Los Angeles to Great Salt Lake" road.

BYU.

58. <u>1859</u>

Explorations of Capt. J. H. Simpson, Corps of Topl. Engrs. U.S.A. in 1859 across the Great Basin of Utah. T. Sinclair, lith. Philadelphia.

23 x 44 cm., ca. 1:3,700,000.

Features Simpson's round trip from Camp Floyd to Genoa and back along the general route of U.S. 50 with the return route often south of the outward route, also Escalante's route of 1776-7 and Fremont's routes.

Wheat 1000.

USU, UHS, BL, LC.

59. <u>1859</u>

Map of Wagon Routes in Utah Territory explored & opened by Capt. J. H. Simpson Topl. Engrs. U.S.A. assisted by Lieuts. J. L. K. Smith and H. S. Putnam Topl. Engrs. U.S.A. and Mr. Henry Engleman in 1858-59 by authority of Hon. John B. Floyd Sec. of War and under instructions from Bvt. Brig. Gen. A. S. Johnston U.S.A. comdg, Dept. of Utah. Drawn by J. P. Mechlin. Explorations of Capt. J. H. Simpson, T. E. U.S.A. in 1859. Facsimile reproduction by The Graphic Co. 39 and 41 Park Place, N.Y.

67 x 122 cm., 1:1,000,000.

Shows roads, trails, and explorers' routes from South Pass to San Francisco. Many place names and elevations shown along Simpson's route and a chart of geographical positions.

Published in <u>Report of Explorations Across the Great Basin of the Territory of Utah for a Direct Wagon Road from Camp Floyd to Genoa in Carson Valley in 1859</u>. Washington, G. P. O., 1876. 35th Cong. 2nd Sess. Sen. Ex. Doc. 40. Serial 984. Superintendent of Documents #W7.5:Si5.

LDSH, UHS, USU, BYU, LC, SUS.

Chapter IV
1860 - 1869

60. <u>1860</u>

Territory and Military Department of Utah compiled in the
Bureau of Topographl. Engrs. of the War Depart. chiefly for military
purposes under the authority of Hon. J. B. Floyd Sec. of War, 1860.
Engraved by W. H. Dougal.

71 x 104 cm., 1:1,500,000.

Roads and explorers' routes are shown in an area bounded by
Denver, Santa Fe, San Francisco, and Los Angeles. Utah's western
boundary is at 116° W. List of authorities includes an 1861 source.
Corrections were made up to January 1862 according to Carl Wheat.

Wheat 1017; Phillips p948.

LDSH, UU, LC, UHS, BYU.

61. <u>1860</u>

Map of Explorations and Surveys in New Mexico and Utah
made under the direction of the Secretary of War by Capt. J. N.
Macomb Topl. Engrs. assisted by C. H. Dimmock, C. Engr. 1860. Let-
tering by John L. Hazard. Geographical Institute, Baron F. W. Von
Egglofstein. No. 164 Broadway, N. York. 1864. Ruling by Samuel
Sartain.

72 x 86 cm. "Scale of 12 miles to 1 inch of 1:760,320."

Features the Four Corners region bounded by Manti, Denver, Flagstaff, and Albuquerque. Relief shown by shading to imitate a plaster model according to Egglofstein. Note in lower right on the "Central Gold Region." Shows routes of Macomb and other explorers.

Published in <u>Report of the Exploring Expedition from Santa Fé, New Mexico, to the Junction of the Grand and Green Rivers of the Great Colorado of the West in 1859 under the Command of Captain J. N. Macomb</u>. Washington, G. P. O., 1876.

Wheat 983.

UU, BL, BYU, LC.

62. <u>1860</u>

Map of the Settlements in the Great Salt Lake Country, Utah.

17.5 x 11.5 cm. colored, 1:1,500,000.

Covers an area from $39°30'$ N. to $42°$ N. and from $111°15'$ W. to $113°15'$ W. Colored by counties. "Cache Sett." is the only settlement in Cache Valley. This map is an inset in the upper right of the "County Map of California."

Found in several Mitchell atlases from 1860 to 1865, variously paged 31, 38, 41, 42, 45, 46.

BL, UHS, BYU, LC.

63. <u>1860</u>

Great Salt Lake City. H. Adlard. sc. London, Longman & Co. 1860. Platted for Cap. Richard F. Burton by Thomas Bullock, G.S.L. City-Utah-Sept. 20, 1860.

20 x 25 cm.

Planimetric map showing lot numbers and major buildings.

Printed in The City of the Saints by Richard F. Burton.
London, Longman Green, Longman and Roberts, 1861, facing p. 240.

BYU, BL.

64. 1860

Colton's Territories of New Mexico and Utah. Published by
Johnson & Browning, 172 William St. New York. Entered . . . 1855
by J. H. Colton.

28 x 36 cm. colored.

Colored by counties. Shows routes explored for railroads.
New Mexico and Arizona are divided horizontally. The Utah-Nevada
border is at 114° W. down to supposed Preuss Lake, then bows to the
east along an unnamed river, across the Wasatch Mountains and down
the Virgin River. Utah counties and names spread across both Utah
and Nevada with a small "Nevada" overprinted.

Colton's General Atlas. New York, Johnson and Browning, 1860,
Entered . . . 1856, 1859 by J. H. Colton, page 51.

LDSH.

65. 1861

Johnson's California, Territories of New Mexico and Utah by
Johnson & Browning.

41 x 62 cm. colored, 1:3,000,000.

"Nevada" is superimposed over the estern half of Utah,
with Utah counties still extending to California. Utah-Nevada border
is at 113°15' W. down the west edge of the Great Salt Lake to Sevier

Lake, then following the course of an unnamed river (Beaver?) past "Vegas de Santa Clara" over the Wasatch Mountains and down the "S. Clara R." to the New Mexico line. Utah extends east to the Continental Divide. The Wasatch Mountains continue the Uintah Mountains as a solid line south and west to the California line south of "Vegas." Fillmore City is the capital. The Emigrant Road, Hastings Road, and the routes of Fremont and Gunnison are shown. New Mexico and Arizona are divided horizontally.

Johnson's New Illustrated (steel plate) Family Atlas, pages 54-55.

Wheat 1027.

BYU, BL.

66. 1861

Johnson's California, Territories of New Mexico and Utah by Johnson & Browning.

40 x 61 cm, colored, 1:3,000,000.

Colored by counties. The Utah-Nevada border is at 116° W. and the Utah-Colorado border at 109° W. Utah county lines extend across Nevada and western Colorado. Name "Nebraska" droops from southern Wyoming into northeast Colorado. The Nevada-California border follows the Sierra Nevada watershed south from Lake Tahoe to 37° N. though the counties are drawn and colored along pre-1861 lines. The Arizona-New Mexico line is horizontal, though not overprinted in red. The Wasatch Range extends unbroken from Brown's Hole to a point southwest of Las Vegas.

Johnson's New Illustrated (steel plate) Family Atlas, pages 54-5.

LDSH, SLP, BYU.

67. <u>1861</u>

Johnson's California, Territories of New Mexico and Utah by Johnson & Browning.

40 x 61 cm. colored, 1:3,000,000.

The Utah-Nevada border is at 116° W. Arizona and New Mexico are divided horizontally at 33°30' N. Shows roads and explorers' routes.

<u>Johnson's New Illustrated (steel plate) Family Atlas.</u> New York, Johnson and Browning, 1861 by J. H. Colton & A. J. Johnson, pages 54-55.

BYU.

68. <u>1861</u>

Map of the Great Salt Lake and adjacent country in the Territory of Utah.

21 x 29 cm. (top half), 1:1,000,000.

Shows the Great Salt Lake and Utah Lake east to Fort Bridger. The only road is from Antelope Island through "G.S.L. Cy." to Utah Valley. The only towns named are Ogden City, G.S.L. Cy., and Ft. Utah (Provo).

The Great Salt Lake (Mormon) City and surrounding country (on an enlarged scale).

21 x 29 cm. (bottom half,) 1:120,000.

Shows the area from Bountiful to Draper with "Welsh Settlement" and "Big Field" featured in the Salt Lake Valley. Based on Stansbury's survey. "G.S.L. Cy." laid out in blocks.

Weekly Dispatch Atlas. 139 Fleet Street, Day & Son Lithrs.
to the Queen. Drawn and Engraved by Edwd. Weller Duke St. Bloomsbury,
page 238.

Phillips 839.

UU, BYU, LC.

69. 1863

Bancroft's map of the Pacific States. Compiled by Wm.
H. Knight. Published by H. H. Bancroft & Co. Booksellers and
Stationers, San Francisco, Cal. 1863. Entered . . . 1863 by
H. H. Bancroft & Co.

151 x 128 cm. colored, 1:1,520,640 or 24 miles to 1 inch.

There is no Idaho, and Arizona is shown with New Mexico
county names. "Proposed route of Central Pacific" railroad is shown
running south of Great Salt Lake. "The Utah of this map is an
achievement, showing towns and villages never previously represented
on a published map, and with many geographical features (like
Strawberry Valley) added." (Wheat 1963, vol. 5, p. 74.) A Table
of distances is off the coast of northern California. An inset of
Hawaiian Group or Sandwich Islands" is off the coast of Oregon and
Washington.

Wheat 1061; Phillips p911.

LC.

70. 1863

Colton's map of California, Nevada, Utah, Colorado, Arizona
and New Mexico. Published by J. H. Colton. 172 William St. New
York. Entered . . . 1855 by J. H. Colton. No. 70.

38 x 62 cm.

Utah's western boundary is at 115° W. Counties are current
to 1863. New Mexico county names written across Arizona. Shows
"Proposed route of Pacific RR," "Mail Route," "Emigrant Road," and
"Hastings Road." "Idaho" is printed across southern Wyoming with
Ft. Hall located on the Medicine Bow River.

Wheat 1064.

UHS.

71. <u>1864</u>

Johnson's California, with Utah, Nevada, Colorado, New
Mexico, and Arizona. Published by Johnson and Ward. Entered . . .
1864 by A. J. Johnson.

40 x 57 cm. colored, 1:3,500,000.

New Mexico counties extend across Arizona even though a
vertical border is printed. Washington is the seat of Washington
County, and Richville is the seat of Tooele County. Shows roads and
overland mail route. Proposed UPRR follows the route of U.S. 50
in western Utah and U.S. 40 in eastern Utah. Proposed CPRR goes
from Pilot Peak north of the Great Salt Lake to Soda Springs and the
South Pass. The Colorado River flows west from its junction with the
San Juan to a point below Harrisville in Washington County.

<u>Johnson's New Illustrated (steel plate) Family Atlas</u>, New
York, Johnson & Ward, 1864, pages 66-67.

Phillips 843.

BYU, LC.

72. <u>1864</u>

Johnson's California, also Utah, Nevada, Colorado, New Mexico, and Arizona. Published by A. J. Johnson, New York. Entered . . . 1864 by A. J. Johnson.

40 x 57 cm. colored, 1:3,000,000.

Colored by counties. Utah's western boundary is at 114° W. Fish Lake is at the head of the Sevier River near the site of Panguitch. No Kane or Rich Counties. The Colorado River enters Arizona at 113° W.

<u>Johnson's New Illustrated (steel plate) Family Atlas.</u> New York, Johnson & Ward, pages 66-67.

Phillips p913; Phillips 843.

USU, BYU, LC.

73. <u>1864</u>

Bancroft's map of the Pacific States. Compiled by Wm. H. Knight. Published by H. H. Bancroft & Co. Booksellers and Stationers, San Francisco, Cal. 1864. Entered . . . 1863 by H. H. Bancroft & Co.

143 x 114 cm. colored, 1:1,520,640, "Scale 24 Statute Miles to an Inch."

A table of distances from San Francisco is off the coast of northern California. Utah's western boundary is at 115° W. Utah counties are shown as of 1863. Shows roads, route of overland mail, and proposed route of Central Pacific Railroad passing south of the Great Salt Lake. There is a large Idaho on one copy and a normal Idaho and a new Montana on another copy.

Wheat 1091; Phillips p912.

BL, BYU, LC.

74. <u>1864</u>

Bancroft's map of California, Nevada, Utah, and Arizona.
Published by H. H. Bancroft & Compy. Booksellers & Stationers,
San Francisco Cal., 1864. Entered . . . 1863 by H. H. Bancroft &
Company.

87 x 72 cm. colored.

Smaller version of "Bancroft's map of the Pacific States."
1864 (Wheat 1091). Wm. H. Knight's name does not appear. The
northern edge is at 42°N. and the eastern edge is at 110° W. There
is no inset of Hawaii.

Wheat 1093.

BL.

75. <u>1864</u>

Colton's Map of the States and Territories West of the
Mississippi River to the Pacific Ocean showing the Overland Routes,
projected Railroad Lines & c. Published by J. H. Colton, No. 172
William St. New York. 1864.

69 x 99 cm. colored, 1:3,200,000.

Utah's western boundary is at 115° W. Counties are current
to 1863. Shows Pony Express route three years after termination.

Wheat 1099; Phillips p913.

BYU, LC.

76. <u>1864</u>

    J. H. Colton's Map of Nevada, Utah, and Arizona.

    27 x 23 cm. colored, 1:4,435,000.

    Colored by counties. The Utah-Nevada border is printed in black at both 116° W. and 115° W., with a red overprint on the 115° W. line. Both Fillmore and G. Salt Lake are marked as capitals. Desert County is named, but without boundaries. San Pete County colored to include eastern Beaver County. Large name "Salt Lake" in Wasatch County.

    <u>Colton's Condensed Octavo Atlas of the Union</u>. New York, J. H. Colton, 1864, pages 41-42.

    Phillips 1387

    BYU, LC.

77. <u>1864</u>

    Colton's Map of the Pacific States, California and Oregon, with the Territories of Nevada, Utah, New Mexico, Colorado & Washington, in connection with British Columbia & c.; from the latest and best information published by J. H. Colton, No. 172 William St. New York, 1864. Entered . . . 1862 by J. H. Colton.

    91 x 68 cm. colored, 1:3,200,000.

    Similar to "Bancroft's map of the Pacific States" of 1864 but with no Montana. Inset of "Map of the Atlantic Ocean showing parts of the Eastern and Western Continents."

    Wheat 1098.

    BL.

78. <u>1865</u>

J. H. Colton's Map of Nevada, Utah, and Arizona.

27 x 23 cm. colored, 1:4,435,000.

County lines and names as of 1862. Utah's western boundary is drawn at 39° W. of Washington, but colored at 38° W. of Washington. Deseret County drawn and named between Elko and Great Salt Lake, but coloring follows new line between Box Elder and Tooele Counties.

<u>Colton's Octavo Atlas of the World</u>. New York, 1865, page 51. Another copy with the Utah-Nevada line at 38° W. of Washington is numbered "26."

BYU, LDSH.

79. <u>1865</u>

County Map of Utah and Nevada. Drawn and Engraved by by (sic) W. H. Gamble Philadelphia. Entered . . . 1865 by S. Augustus Mitchell, Jr.

26 x 32 cm. colored, 1:3,000,000.

No Kane, Piute, Sevier, or Rich Counties shown. Shows Hastings Road, Telegraph Route, roads, and minining districts in Nevada. Colored by counties. Utah's western border is at 115° W. Preuss Lake is in western Beaver County.

<u>Mitchell's New General Atlas</u>. Philadelphia, S. D. Mitchell, 1866, page 33.

Phillips 848.

UHS, SLP, BYU, LC, SUS.

80. <u>1865</u>

Utah.

27 x 18 cm.

No counties are shown, but some roads and trails are shown including a long abandoned Spanish Trail and "New Overland Mail Route" across Uintah Basin and Strawberry Valley to Springville. Of particular note is the defunct Pony Express Trail with all stations named west to 115°W.

Published in <u>State, Territorial & Ocean Guide Book of the Pacific</u> by Sterling M. Holdredge. Chromolith, Grafton T. Brown, 543 Clay St. S. F. 1865, 1866.

Wheat 1123.

81. <u>1866</u>

Bancroft's Map of the Rocky Mountain States, and the Pacific Coast. Compiled by Wm. H. Knight. Published by H. H. Bancroft & Company, Booksellers & Stationers. San Francisco Cal. 1866. Entered . . . 1865 by H. H. Bancroft & Company.

42 x 48 cm.

Reduced from the 1863 and 1864 editions with less detail.

Wheat 1132; Phillips p914.

LC.

82. <u>1866</u>

Territory and Military Department of Utah compiled in the Bureau of Topographical Engrs. of the War Departt. chiefly for Military purposes. Under the authority of the Hon. J. B. Floyd. Sec. of War. 1860. Julius Bien & Co. Lith. N.Y.

42 x 62 cm. colored, 1:2,500,000.

"Authorities" list sources up to 1866. Shows roads and explorers' routes. Military posts are shown in blue with Fort Bridger the only post in Utah.

Atlas to Accompany the Official Records of the Union and Confederate Armies 1861-1865. Washington, G.P.O., 1892. Plate CXX.

Phillips 1353.

USU, UHS, LC, SUS.

83. 1866

Map of the Southern Pacific States.

28 x 44 cm. colored, 1:4,752,000 or 75 miles to 1 inch.

Colored by counties. Richland and Kane counties are shown, but not Sevier and Piute.

Clark's New School Geography by Charles Russell Clark, San Francisco, H. H. Bancroft, 1866.

LDSH.

84. 1866

Map of the Territory of Utah. To accompany the annual Report of the Commissioner of the General Land Office. Department of the Interior. General Land Office. October 2nd 1866. (signed) _____ Nelson, Commissioner. Scale 18 Miles to an Inch. The Major & Knapp Engraving, Manuf'g. & Lithographic Company. 71 Broadway, New York.

64 x 46 cm. colored, 1:1,000,000.

The title is at the bottom. Shows reservations, also gold, iron, and lead deposits. There is a large gold deposit indicated along

the north bank of the San Juan River. Rich, Sevier, and Piute
counties are not shown. There is a mountain range running vertically
through the Salt Flats. Shows roads, explorers' routes, and township
lines.

Wheat 1155; Hargett 786; Phillips 1388.

LDSH, USU, UU, BYU, LC, BL.

85. 1866

Johnson's California, also Utah, Nevada, Colorado, New
Mexico and Arizona. Published by A. J. Johnson, New York.
Entered . . . 1864 by A. J. Johnson.

40 x 57 cm. colored, 1:3,500,000.

Shows 1866 details such as the Utah-Nevada border at 114° W.,
but no Rich County. "Union Pacific RR" shown along the old mail
route east of Salt Lake City.

Johnson's New Illustrated Family Atlas of the World. New
York, A. J. Johnson, 1866, pages 66-67.

Phillips 4346.

BYU, LC.

86. 1867

National map of the Territory of the United States from the
Mississippi River to the Pacific Ocean. Made by the authority of
the Hon. O. H. Browning Secretary of the Interior. In the Office of
the Indian Bureau chiefly for government purposes under the direction
of the Hon. N. G. Taylor Commisr. of Indian Affairs & Hon. Chas.
E. Mix Chief Clerk of the Indian Bureau. Compiled from authorized

explorations of Pacific Rail Road Routes, Public Surveys, and other
reliable data from the Departments of the Government at Washington,
D.C. by W. J. Keeler, Civil Engineer. 1867. N. DuBois Draughtsman.
J. L. Gedney, Lithographer, Engraver & Plate Printer, Washington, D.C.

    121 x 145 cm. colored, 1:2,280,960 or 36 miles to 1 inch.

    Shows Indian reservations, railroads completed and in pro-
gress and some township lines. Gold, silver, copper, quicksilver,
iron and coal deposits color coded. Copyrighted by Keeler, yet
printed by the G. P. O.

    Wheat 1170; Phillips p916.

    BYU, LC.

87. <u>1867</u>

    Map of the Settlements in the Great Salt Lake Country, Utah.
17.5 x 11.5 cm. colored, 1:1,500,000.

    Colored by counties. Covers area from $39^{\circ}30'$ N. to 42° N.
and from $111^{\circ}15'$ W. to $113^{\circ}15$; W. Printed as an inset in the upper
right of "County Map of California." Many new settlements shown in
Cache Valley.

    <u>Mitchell's New General Atlas</u>. Philadelphia, S. Augustus
Mitchell. Found in editions copyrighted 1860, 1866, 1867, and paged
52 or 56.

    BYU, LC.

88. <u>1867</u>

    County Map of Utah and Nevada. Drawn and Engraved by by
(sic) W. H. Gamble, Philadelphia. Entered . . . 1867 by S. Augustus
Mitchell Jr.

26 x 33 cm. colored, 1:3,000,000.

Central Pacific Railroad shown completed with a branch projected to Salt Lake City. Kane County shown, but not Piute, Sevier, or Rich. No Wyoming indicated yet. Colored by counties.

Mitchell's New General Atlas. Philadelphia, S. A. Mitchell, 1868, page 52.

Wheat 1205; Phillips 3563a.

Another copy showing state and county lines as of 1863, no railroads completed or projected, but showing the overland mail route and telegraph route and numbered "49."

Another copy including Kane County and showing the "Central Pacific RR" completed to Wadsworth, Nevada and a projected railroad north of the Great Salt Lake, then down to the top of Promontory Point and across Bear River Bay to Ogden and eastward.

BYU, UHS, LC, BL.

89. 1867

Map Showing the Route of the Central Pacific Railroad from San Francisco to the Mississippi River. Published by G. W. and C. B. Colton & Co. 172 William St. New York, 1867. Entered . . . 1867 by G. W. and C. B. Colton & Co.

44 x 101 cm.

Shows Utah county boundaries as of 1863 and state lines as of 1866. Shows route of "Central Pacific RR" around north end of Great Salt Lake meeting the "Union Pacific RR" at the mouth of Echo Canyon.

Wheat 1166.

90. 1867

Bancroft's Map of the Pacific States. Compiled by Wm. Henry Knight. Published by H. H. Bancroft & Co. Booksellers and Stationers, San Francisco Cal. 1867. Entered . . . 1867 by H. H. Bancroft & Co.

153 x 125 cm. colored.

Shows existing railroads (none in Utah) and existing wagon roads. Drainage system for southeast Utah surprisingly accurate. A large Preuss Lake still depicted south of Sevier Lake and fed by the lower Beaver River. Wyoming still part of Dakota. Tables of "Distances from San Francisco" and "Facts and Statistics" located off the coast. No inset of Hawaii.

Phillips p915.

BL, LC.

91. 1868

Head Quarters Corps of Engineers War Department. Territory of the United States from the Mississippi River to the Pacific Ocean; originally prepared to accompany the Reports of the Explorations for a Pacific Railroad Route; made in accordance with the 10th & 11th sections of the Army Appropriation Act of March 3rd 1853; compiled from authorized explorations and other reliable data by Lieut. G. K. Warren, Top'l Eng'rs, in the office of the Pacific RR Surveys, War Dept. under the direction of Bvt Maj. W. H. Emory, Top'l Eng'rs. in 1854. Capt. A. A. Humphreys, Top'l Eng'rs. in 1854-58. Recompiled and redrawn under the direction of the Chief of Corps of Engineers by Edward Freyhold 1865-66-67-68. Julius Bien, New York.

122 x 186 cm.

Based on G. K. Warren's monumental map of 1857, very detailed with much updating, showing roads and railroads. Inset of "Territory of Alaska ceded by Russia to the United States 1868." Includes a long list of authorities.

Wheat 1185; Phillips p904, p917.

UU, LC.

92. <u>1868</u>

Bancroft's Map of California, Nevada, Utah and Arizona. San Francisco. H. H. Bancroft & Co., 1868. Entered . . . 1867 by H. H. Bancroft & Company.

78 x 102 cm. colored, 1:1,520,640 or 24 miles to 1 inch.

Taken off the plate for "Bancroft's map of the Pacific States."

Wheat 1178.

BL.

93. <u>1868</u>

Bancroft's map of the Pacific States. Compiled by Wm. Henry Knight. Published by H. H. Bancroft & Co. Booksellers and Stationers. San Francisco, Cal. 1868. Entered . . . 1867 by H. H. Bancroft & Company.

143 x 115 cm. colored, 1:1,520,640 or 24 miles to 1 inch.

Lack of change in status of railroad construction or creation of Wyoming Territory indicate no updating of the third edition of 1867.

Wheat 1176.

BL.

94. <u>1868</u>

California, Oregon, Idaho, Utah, Nevada, Arizona, and
Washington.

28 x 21 cm.

Name of Great Salt Lake City officially changed to Salt Lake
City that year and noted. No Preuss Lake or Sevier, Piute, and Rich
counties shown. "Pacific Railroad Route" shown coming south of Great
Salt Lake. The Union Pacific Railroad goes north of Great Salt
Lake to the site of Wells, Nevada.

<u>Mitchell's New Reference Atlas</u>. Philadelphia, S. Augustus
Mitchell, plate XIX.

Wheat 1188.

BL.

95. <u>1869</u>

Map showing detailed topography of the country traversed by
the reconnaissance expedition through southern & southeastern Nevada
in charge of Lieut. Geo. M. Wheeler U.S. Engineers. Assisted by
Lieut. D. W. Lockwood Corps of Engineers U.S.A. 1869. P. W. Hamel
Chief Topographer and draughtsman. Photolith by the N. Y. Lithg.
& Prtg. Co. 16 & 18 Park Place. Reconnaissance maps Department of
California. Military Map No. 1.

94 x 52 cm., 1:760,320 or "Scale 1 inch to 12 miles."

Covers area from White Pine district to the Colorado River.
Great detail in Utah from Sevier Lake west. Wheeler discovered that
Preuss Lake was a myth and not to be confused with Sevier Lake.

Wheat 1218.

BYU, USU, BL.

96. <u>1869</u>

Colton's map of California, Nevada, Utah, Colorado, Arizona, and New Mexico. Published by G. W. and C. B. Colton & Co. No. 172 William St. New York. Entered . . . 1865 by G. W. and C. B. Colton & Co.

38 x 64 cm. colored.

Similar to the 1863 edition. Wyoming is named but Ft. Hall is still shown to be on the Medicine Bow River. Shows the Pahranagat Mines in Nevada, but not the White Pine District.

<u>Colton's General Atlas</u>, pages 80-81.

Wheat 1200.

BL.

97. <u>1869</u>

Plat of Salt Lake City. Lith. by Chas. Shover & Co. Chicago.

30 x 41 cm., ca. 1:19,500.

Shows section and quarter section lines; blocks are numbered, lots drawn in, and streets named.

Published in <u>Gazeteer of Utah and Salt Lake City</u> by Edward L. Sloan. 1869.

UU.

98. <u>1869</u>

Map of Utah and Colorado. Prepared by order of Lieut. Genl. W. T. Sherman. Bvt. Maj. Genl. A. A. Humphreys Chief of Engineers. Compiled under direction of Bvt. Col. Wm. E. Merrill. Maj. Engrs.

St. Louis, 1869. Drawn by H. DeWerthern, R. P. Studley & Co. lith.
St. Louis, Mo.

66 x 114 cm., 1:1,200,000.

Printed on linen for use in the field. List of authorities
in lower left. Shows railroads, wagon roads, trails, explorers'
routes, railroad surveys, and military posts.

Hargett 131.

LDSH, LC.

99. 1869

Map of the Union Pacific Rail Road and Surveys of 1864, 65,
66, 67, 1868 from Missouri River to Humboldt Wells. Grenville M.
Dodge, Chief Engineer. H. Lambach del. January, 1869.

53 x 165 cm.

Below the map is a "Profile of Grades." Many explorations
off the main line are traced. The line is shown completed to
Humboldt Wells though the actual track ended at Echo. Utah is shown
from Nephi to Franklin.

Wheat 1209.

WCL, LC.

Chapter V
1870 - 1879

100. <u>1870</u>

Map of the Territory of Utah. B. A. M. Froiseth. 1870.
Am. photo-Lithographic Co. N.Y. (Osbornes Process).

25 x 17 cm. colored, 1:2,900,000.

Counties colored including Rio Virgin County. "Fort
Roubedon" is located at the confluence of the Green and White Rivers.
Shows roads, trails, explorers' routes, railroads, and proposed
railroads.

Great Salt Lake Valley. B. A. M. Froiseth. 1869.

15 x 10 cm. colored, 1:1,267,200 or 20 miles to 1 inch.

Colored by counties.

Plat of Salt Lake City, Utah. B. A. M. Froiseth. 1870.

15 x 11.5 cm. colored, ca. 1:50,000.

Salt Lake City colored by wards. All three maps on one sheet
38 x 31 cm. There is a portrait of Brigham Young in the lower right
signed "Correct Brigham Young."

Another edition published by the Skandinavisk Post in New
York, 1870.

Phillips p948.

LC, BL, UHS, SLP, LDSH, UU, BYU.

101. <u>1870</u>

Map of Utah to accompany Beadle's History of the Mormons.
F. Bourguin Lith. Phila.

21 x 22 cm., 1:3,000,000.

Shows roads and railroads with a branch under construction
from Ogden to Salt Lake City. There are no Piute, Sevier, or Rich
counties.

LDSH, SUS.

102. <u>1870</u>

Bird's Eye View of Salt Lake City, Utah Territory 1870.
Drawn by Augustus Koch. Chicago Lithographing Co. No. 150, 152, &
154, S. Clark St. Chicago, Ill.

46 x 61 cm.

Oblique aerial view from the southwest over the corner of 8th
South and 5th West. There is a procession of carriages coming up 1st
East. The Tabernacle and the Temple are shown completed. There is a
railroad coming down 4th West to a terminal between North and South
Temple. There are eight views of buildings inset in lower corners.
Forty-nine points of interest are numbered and listed.

Herbert 928.

UU, UHS, BYU, LC.

103. <u>1870</u>

Part of the U.S. Engineer Department's Map of the Western
States and Territories Showing Location of Mining Districts. Plate I.

35 x 58 cm. colored, 1:2,900,000.

Derived from the 1868 map of Edward Freyhold. Mining districts are underlined in red. None are in Utah. A publication of Clarence King's Fortieth Parallel Survey.

Atlas Accompanying Volume III on Mining Industry. United States Geological Exploration of the Fortieth Parallel, Clarence King Geologist in Charge. Plate I. Engraved and Printed by Julius Bien, New York. 1876. Superintendent of Documents # W 7.10:18.

Wheat 1215; Phillips 1279.

BYU, LC.

104. 1870

Bancroft's map of the Pacific States. Compiled by Wm. Henry Knight Published by H. H. Bancroft & Co. Booksellers and Stationers. San Francisco Cal. 1870. Joseph Laing Lith., 107 Fulton St. N.Y. Entered . . . 1867 by H. H. Bancroft & Company.

141 x 113 cm. colored, 1:1,520,640 or 24 miles to 1 inch.

Shows completed railroads, proposed railroads, and military posts of which there are three in Utah: a Ft. Crittenden at Fairfield, Ft. Gunnison, and a Ft. Union north of Fillmore. There is still a Preuss Lake ten miles south of Sevier Lake connected with it and the same size. There is a table of distances from San Francisco printed off the northern coast of California. "Territory of Alaska" is inset off the mouth of the Columbia. "Pacific and Atlantic Railroad map of the United States" is in the lower left.

Other issues are 156 x 128 cm. and 113 x 76 cm.

Wheat 1210.

BYU.

105. <u>1870</u>

County Map of Utah and Nevada. Drawn and Engraved by by (sic) W. H. Gamble, Philadelphia. Entered . . . 1870 by S. Augustus Mitchell Jr.

26 x 32 cm. colored, 1:3,000,000.

Colored by counties. Green River County has gone to Wyoming. Kane County is shown but not Piute, Sevier, or Rich. The railroad from Ogden to Salt Lake City is completed. Shows roads, railroads, and mining districts in Nevada.

<u>Mitchell's New General Atlas</u>, page 52. Another copy gives Green River County to Utah, and the railroad spur to Salt Lake City is under construction.

UU, BYU, SUS.

106. <u>1870</u>

Johnson's California also Utah, Nevada, Colorado, New Mexico, and Arizona. Published by A. J. Johnson, New York. Entered . . . 1864 by A. J. Johnson.

39 x 56 cm. colored, 1:3,500,000.

Some information such as railroads is updated to 1869.

<u>Johnson's New Illustrated Family Atlas</u>. New York, 1870, pages 79-80.

Phillips 858.

BYU, LC.

107. <u>1871</u>

Bancroft's Map of California, Nevada, Utah, and Arizona. Published by A. L. Bancroft & Compy. Booksellers & Stationers

San Francisco Cal. 1871.

    71 x 80 cm. colored, 1:1,520,640 or 24 miles to 1 inch.

    Southern half of "Bancroft's Map of the Pacific States," 1870. Re-issued in 1873, 1876 (Phillips p186), and 1878 with little change except the extent of the railroads.

    Wheat 1219.

    BL.

108. <u>1871</u>

    Crofutt's New Map of Salt Lake City, Utah. Drawn by B. A. M. Froiseth. Expressly for Crofutt's Trans Continental Tourists Guide. New York, engraved by the Actinic Engraving Co.

    24 x 33 cm.

    Blocks, wards and streets named and numbered to 9th South. Twenty-five points of interest are numbered and listed.

    Phillips p772.

    SLP, LC.

109. <u>1871</u>

    Map of Salt Lake City and suburbs. Published by John L. Burns, Salt Lake City, Utah. 1871.

    Colored, 1:15,840 or 4 miles to 1 inch.

    Colored by wards; gives section numbers, street names, block numbers, and lot numbers with a list of references.

    Phillips p772.

    LDSH, BYU, LC.

110. 1871

New Mining Map of Utah. Showing the location of the Mining
Districts over an extent of Territory 150 miles from North to
South. Compiled from U.S. Government Surveys and Other Authentic
Sources by B. A. M. Froiseth. Aided by H. R. Durkee Salt Lake City
1871. New York. American photo lith. co. (Osborne's process).

80 x 52 cm., 1:253,440.

Shows an area from Tintic to Logan and from Echo to the
western shore of Great Salt Lake. Covers the same area as Stansbury's
map. There are insets of the City of Alta, Eureka City, City of
Stockton, and Ophir. Mercur is called "Silverapols." There are
advertisements around the border. The railroad has advanced south to
Payson. Shows townships, roads, railroads, villages, and mining
districts.

Wheat 1223; Phillips p948.

LDSH, UU, LC, SLP, UHS, BYU.

111. 1871

Froiseth's New Sectional & Mineral Map of Utah, compiled from
the latest U.S. Government Surveys and other authentic sources.
Exhibiting the Sections, Fractional Sections, Counties, Cities,
Towns, Settlements, Mines, Railroads, and other Internal Improvements.
Published by B. A. M. Froiseth, Salt Lake City, Utah, 1871. A. L.
Bancroft & Co. Lith. 721 Market St. San Francisco.

134 x 88 cm. colored; 1:506,880 or 8 miles to 1 inch.

At the bottom are plans of the City of Corinne, City of St.
George, Provo City, Salt Lake City, Ogden City, Logan City, and City

of Stockton. The steamboat route from Lake Point to Corinne is illustrated with two steamboats. The Utah Southern Railroad reaches south to Payson. There is a scroll with population figures and references on the Kaiparowitz Plateau. The junction of the Colorado and San Juan is "supposed." A large Sierra Tucane is northeast of Paria and Navajo Mountain is called Sierra Panoche. Mineral resources are shown by type including coal deposits on Provo Peak. There is a large Fish Lake at Brighton. This is the first map to show a "Proposed Denver Pacific Railroad."

Wheat 1224; Phillips p948.

UHS, BYU, BL, LC.

112. <u>1871</u>

Colton's California, Nevada, Utah, Colorado, Arizona, & New Mexico. Published by G. W. and C. B. Colton & Co. No 172 William St. New York.

40 x 64 cm. colored, 1:3,000,000.

Information is generally dated 1864 to 1869. There is a large Preuss Lake, no Piute or Sevier counties, and an important White Pine District in Nevada. The Colorado River canyons are named according to the Powell expeditions.

<u>Colton's General Atlas</u>, pages 80-81.

BYU.

113. <u>1872</u>

County Map of Utah and Nevada. Drawn and Engraved by by (sic) W. H. Gamble, Philadelphia. Entered . . . 1872 by S. Augustus Mitchell.

25 x 32 cm. colored, 1:3,000,000.

A large Preuss Lake is entirely in Nevada. Colored by counties, including Rio Virgin County. Evanston is in Summit County. Utah Southern Railroad is completed to Payson. Eastern Summit county above the Uintah Mountains is marked and colored as a separate but unnamed county.

Mitchell's New General Atlas, page 48. Another copy is page 52 from an 1875 edition of the atlas.

UU, UHS, BYU, SUS.

114. 1873

Asher & Adams portions of Utah, Colorado, and Wyoming. Entered . . . 1872 by Asher & Adams.

40 x 57 cm. colored, 1:1,267,200 or 20 miles to 1 inch.

Northern Utah down to Monroe is inset 30 x 32 cm. on a map of Colorado and southern Wyoming. Colored by counties; shows railroads and townships.

Asher & Adams New Commercial, Topographical and Statistical Atlas and Gazetteer of the United States, pages 107-108.

Phillips p920.

BYU, UU, LDSH, SLP, SUS, LC.

115. 1873

Asher & Adams Utah. 1873.

40 x 50 cm. colored, 1:1,267,200 or 20 miles to 1 inch.

Utah Southern Railroad is completed to Payson and projected to Iron County and Pioche railroad is also projected from Sandy through Alta City to Heber. Washington and Kane counties are cut off.

Nephi is called "Salt Creek." Some copies have railroads to two different Pioches and an inset of "South West Portion of Utah" in the lower right.

Phillips p948.

BYU, LC, UHS, UU.

116. <u>1873</u>

Froiseth's Map of Little Cottonwood Mining District and Vicinity, Salt Lake County, Utah. Compiled from the latest United States Surveys and other authentic sources. Exhibiting the Mines which have been surveyed for U.S. Patent, and locations of other mines. By B. A. M. Froiseth, Salt Lake City. 1873. A. M. Photo-Lithographic Co. N.Y. (Osbornes Process).

62 x 81 cm. colored, 1:4800 or 400 feet to 1 inch.

Shows mines, tunnels, and roads. The streets are named and blocks numbered for Alta City and Central City. Includes note "The mines surveyed for patent are correctly represented on the above map. (signed) C. C. Clement, U.S. Surveyor General for Utah."

UU.

117. <u>1873</u>

Map Showing the route of the Salt Lake, Sevier Valley, and Pioche Railroad. Compiled from official surveys of the United States government and late explorations and surveys by the company's engineers. H. Carmer Hopper del. E. Wells Sackett & Bro. 56 & 58 William St. N. Y.

61 x 38 cm. colored, 1:1,000,000.

Shows mining districts, township lines, with railroads completed to Provo and Stockton and proposed from Stockton to Iron Springs and Pioche.

LDSH.

118. 1873

Utah. 1873. O. W. Gray & Son.

36 x 29 cm. colored, 1:1,584,000.

Colored by counties. Railroads are shown to Tooele, Santaquin, Alta, Silver Lake City in American Fork Canyon, Coalville, and Franklin. "Gray's" Idaho, Montana, and Wyoming on the verso.

Atlas of the United States, Philadelphia, Stedman, Brown, & Lyon, 1873, page 116.

Phillips p922; Phillips 1390.

Another copy is titled "Gray's Atlas Utah 1873" with railroads completed to Springville, Coalville, up American Fork Canyon, Bingham, Franklin, and projected to Pioche by way of Tooele and Deseret and to Fillmore from Springville by way of Nephi.

Phillips 4526.

UU, UHS, GSL, BL, LC, SUS.

119. 1873

(Pacific States) California, Nevada, Oregon, Washington, Idaho, Utah, Arizona, and part of Montana. T. Ellwood Zell, Philadelphia. Engraved & Printed in Colour by J. Bartholomew.

48 x 29 cm. colored, 1:5,100,000.

Shows counties, towns, and railroads, including Rio Virgin County.

A Descriptive Hand Atlas of the World. Philadelphia, T.
Ellwood Zell, 1873.

Phillips 865.

BYU, LC.

120. 1873

Green River from the Union Pacific Railroad to the Mouth of
the White River. 1873. Map A. Department of the Interior. U. S.
Geological and Geographical Survey of the Territories. Second
Division. J. W. Powell, Geologist in charge. A. H. Thompson, Geographer. H. C. DeMotte & F. M. Bishop, Topographers. W. H. Graves
del.

73 x 48 cm. colored, 1:253,440 or "Scale 4 miles to 1 inch."
Covers area from 40°03' N, to 41°40' N. and from 108°30' W. to
109°52' W. Relief shown by contours with contour interval 250 feet.
One copy colored to show land usage: irrigable lands, pine lands,
cottonwood groves, copper and silver region. Another copy colored to
show geology.

Atlas accompanying the report on the Geology of a portion of
the Uintah Mountains and a region of country adjacent thereto.
by J. W. Powell, Geologist in Charge. 1876. Julius Bien Lith.
Superintendent of Documents #I17.2:Ui5.

Wheat 1274; Phillips 2590.

Also published in Exploration of the Colorado River of the
West and Its Tributaries. Explored in 1869, 1870, 1871, and 1872
under the direction of the Secretary of the Smithsonian Institution.
Washington. 1875. 43rd Cong. 1st Sess. House Misc. Doc. 300.

Serial 1622 with a shortened title: "Green River from the Union Pacific Railroad to the Mouth of the White River. 1873."

Wheat 1261; Schmeckebier p 39-40; Phillips 2590.

BYU, LC.

121. <u>1874</u>

Map of the Territory of Utah. Entered . . . 1874 by B. A. M. Froiseth. Am. Photo-Lithographic Co. N. Y. (Osborne's process).

26 x 17 cm. colored, 1:2,900,000.

Colored by counties including Rio Virgin County. Shows explorers' routes.

Great Salt Lake Valley. Entered . . . 1874 by B. A. M. Froiseth. Am. Photo-Lithographic Co. N. Y. (Osborne's process).

16 x 10 cm. colored, 1:1,230,000.

Colored by counties. Shows roads, railroads, and townships.

Plat of Salt Lake City, Utah. Entered . . . 1874 by B. A. M. Froiseth. Am. Photo-Lithograhpic Co. N. Y. (Osborne's process).

16 x 12 cm. colored, ca. 1:50,000.

Colored by wards with twelve points of interest numbered and listed.

Three maps on sheet 38 x 31 cm. with a portrait of Brigham Young in the lower right signed "Correct Brigham Young."

SLP.

127. <u>1874</u>

Colton's Utah & Colorado. Published by G. W. and C. B. Colton and Co. No. 172 William St. New York.

29 x 36 cm. colored, 1:3,000,000.

Colored by counties. Eastern Kansas is on the verso.
Railroads are shown completed to Payson and Franklin, and proposed to
Pioche and across Uintah Basin. Evanston is in Utah on the Summit and
Morgan County line. Piute, Kane, and Rich counties are shown, but
not Sevier County. The south end of Bear Lake barely reaches the
Utah line.

Colton's General Atlas. New York, G. W. & C. B. Colton
1874. Entered . . . 1863 by J. H. Colton, page 82.

Phillips 3564.

LDSH, UHS, LC.

123. 1874

Map of the Pacific States and Territories. Published by
Taintor Bros. & Merrill. New York.

66 x 47 cm. colored, 1:3,168,000 or "Fifty miles to an inch."

Railroads are shown completed to Payson, Franklin, and up
American Fork Canyon.

The American Household and Commercial Atlas of the World.
New York, Taintor Bros. & Merrill, 1874. No. XXXVI, XXXVIA.

Phillips 872.

BYU, LC.

124. 1874

Utah.

38 x 30 cm. colored, 1:1,584,000 or 25 miles to 1 inch.

Colored by counties. Marysvale is called "Maysville."
Railroads are shown projected to the vicinity of Black Rock by way of

Nephi and Fillmore and to Pioche by way of Tooele, Deseret, and Iron
Springs. The Kaiparowits Plateau region is labeled "Broken Alkaline
Mountains (unexplored)."

Atlas of the United States, Philadelphia, Frank Gray, 1874,
page 143. Another copy titled "Gray's Atlas Utah 1873."

BYU, UHS, SUS.

125. 1874

Geographical Explorations & Surveys West of the 100th
Meridian. Central & Western Utah Atlas Sheet No. 50. Expeditions
of 1872 & 1873 Under the Command of 1st Lieut. Geo. M. Wheeler, Corps
of Engineers. By Order of the Honorable Wm. M. Belknap, Secretary
of War. Under the Direction of Brig. Gen. A. A. Humphreys, Chief of
Engineers, U.S. Army. Weyess, Herman & Aguirre Del.

38 x 48 cm. colored, "Scale: 1 inch to 8 miles or 1:506,880."
Shows from 39° N. to $40^\circ 40'$ N. and from 111° W. to $113^\circ 40'$ W.
Shows roads, trails, railroads, and telegraph lines with mileage.

Issued in three hachured, one shaded, and one geologic
edition listing "G. K. Gilbert, A. R. Marvine, E. E. Howell, Geological
Assistants."

Described in Schmeckebier's Catalogue, pages 60-65, and
Wheeler's Geographical Report, pages 252-255.

BYU, UU, UHS, LC.

126. 1874

Explorations & Surveys West of the One-Hundredth Meridian.
Parts of Eastern & Southeastern Nevada & Southwestern Utah. Atlas

Sheet Number 58. Expeditions of 1869, 1871, & 1872, Under the Command
of 1st Lieut. Geo. M. Wheeler, Corps of Engineers, U.S. Army. By
Order of the Honorable Wm. M. Belknap, Secretary of War. Under the
Direction of Brig. Gen. A. A. Humphreys, Chief of Engineers, U.S.
Army. Weyess, Herman & Aguirre Del.

37 x 49 cm. colored, "Scale 1 inch to 8 miles or 1:506,880."

Shows area from $37^{\circ}20'$ N. to 39° N. and from $113^{\circ}45'$ W. to
$116^{\circ}30'$ W. Shows roads, railroads, trails, and telegraph lines with
mileage.

Issued in three hachured, one shaded, and one geologic
edition on a sheet with a portion of No. 66.

Described in Wheeler's Geographical Report, pages 265-267, and
Schmeckebier's Catalogue, pages 60-65.

LDSH, BYU, UU, LC.

127. 1874

Explorations & Surveys West of the One-Hundredth Meridian.
Southeastern Utah. Atlas Sheet Number 59. Expeditions of 1872
& 1873 Under the Command of 1st Lieut. Geo. M. Wheeler, Corps of
Engineers, U.S. Army. By Order of the Honorable Wm. M. Belknap,
Secretary of War. Under the Direction of Brig. Gen. A. A. Humphreys,
Chief of Engineers, U. S. Army. Weyss, Herman & Aguirre, Del.

38 x 40 cm. colored, "Scale 1 inch to 8 miles or 1:506,880."

Shows from $37^{\circ}20'$ N. to 39° N. and from 111° W. to $113^{\circ}45'$ W.
Shows roads, trails, railroads, and telegraph lines with mileage.

Issued in five hachured, one shaded, and one geologic edition
with "G. K. Gilbert, A. R. Marvine, E. E. Howell, Geological Assistants."

Described in Wheeler's <u>Geographical Report</u>, pages 267-270, and Schmeckebier's <u>Catalogue</u>, pages 60-65.

LDSH, UU, BYU, LC.

128. <u>1874</u>

Explorations & Surveys West of the One-Hundredth Meridian. Parts of Eastern & South-eastern Nevada & South-western Utah. Atlas Sheet No. 66. Expeditions of 1869, 1871, & 1872, under the Command of 1st Lieut. Geo M. Wheeler, Corps of Engineers, U. S. Army. By Order of the Honorable the Secretary of War. Under the Direction of Brig. Gen. A. A. Humphreys, Chief of Engineers, U.S. Army. Weyss, Herman, & Lang, Del.

37 x 50 cm. colored, "Scale 1 inch to 8 miles or 1:506,880."

Shows roads, trails, and telegraph lines with mileage. Shows from $35^{\circ}40'$ N. to $37^{\circ}20'$ N. and from 111° W. to $113^{\circ}45'$ W.

Issued in one hachured, one shaded, and one geologic edition with "G. K. Gilbert, A. R. Marvine, E. E. Howell, Geological Assistants."

Described in Wheeler's <u>Geographical Report</u>, pages 283-286, and Schmeckebier's <u>Catalogue</u>, pages 60-65.

LDSH, BYU, UU, LC.

129. <u>1874</u>

Map of the Territory of Utah. Showing the extent and progress of the Public Surveys. To accompany Annual Report of the Surveyor General 1874. Scale: 8 miles to one Inch. Surveyor General's Office, Salt Lake City, Utah, November 25th 1874. (signed) Nathan Kimball. Surv. Genl. B. A. M. Froiseth, Draughtsman.

126 x 97 cm., 1:506,880.

This is Froiseth's map with a different title and no city plans at the bottom. Mineral resources are included. A scroll with population figures and references is printed in San Juan County.

Hargett 787.

BYU, LC.

130. <u>1875</u>

U. S. Geographical Surveys West of the 100th Meridian. Parts of Northern & North-western Arizona & Southern Utah. Atlas Sheet No. 67. Expeditions of 1871, 1872, & 1873 under the command of 1st Lieut. Geo. M. Wheeler, Corps of Engineers, U. S. Army. By Order of the Honorable the Secretary of War. Under the Direction of Brig. Gen. A. A. Humphreys, Chief of Engineers, U. S. Army. Weyss, Herman & Lang, Del.

37 x 50 cm. colored, "Scale 1 inch to 8 miles or 1:506,880."

Shows roads, trails and telegraph lines with mileage.

Shows from $35°40'$ N. to $37°20'$ N and from $111°$ W. to $113°45'$ W.

Issued in one hachured, one shaded, and one geologic edition with "G. K. Gilbert, A. R. Marvine, E. E. Howell, Geologic Assistants."

Described in Wheeler's <u>Geographical Report</u>, pages 283-286, and Schmekebier's <u>Catalogue</u>, pages 60-65.

LDSH, BYU, UU, LC.

131. <u>1875</u>

Froiseth's New Sectional & Mineral Map of Utah. Compiled from the latest U. S. Government Surveys and other authentic sources.

Exhibiting the Sections, Fractional Sections, Counties, Cities, Towns, Settlements, Mining Districts, Railroads, and other Internal Improvements. Published by B. A. M. Froiseth, Salt Lake City, 1875. A. L. Bancroft & Co. Lith. S. F. Second Edition thoroughly revised, re-engraved, and brought down to date.

134 x 88 cm. colored, 1:506,880.

Along the bottom are insets of City of Corinne, St. George, Provo City, Salt Lake City, Ogden City, Logan City, and City of Stockton. A scroll on the Kaiparowits Plateau has a legend and population table. Henry Mountains are called "Dirty Devil Mountains." There is much more detail and place names along the Colorado River, reflecting Powell's explorations. Another copy has the scroll centered in San Juan County; the City of Corinne is replaced by Brigham City and the City of Stockton is replaced by Coalville.

Wheat 1254; Phillips p948.

BYU, SLP, LC, BL.

132. <u>1875</u>

Johnson's California, also Utah, Nevada, Colorado, New Mexico, and Arizona, published by Alvin J. Johnson & Son, New York. Entered . . . 1864 by A. J. Johnson.

40 x 57 cm. colored, 1:3,420,000.

Colored by counties. Revision to 1875 is indicated by the inclusion of Pinal County, Arizona.

<u>Johnson's New Illustrated Family Atlas.</u> New York, A. J. Johnson.

BYU.

133. <u>1875</u>

Watson's New County and Railroad Map of the Pacific States. Published by D. Needham, No. 613 Mission Street, San Francisco, California, 1875. Entered . . . 1874 by Gaylord Watson. Engraved by Louis E. Neuman, 36 Vesey St. New York.

97 x 67 cm. colored, 1:2,000,000.

Colored by counties. Piute and Sevier counties are missing. Rich county is "Richland" and San Pete is "Pete." Panguitch is called "Panguish" and Kanab is called "Kanash." Railroads are shown completed to Provo and Franklin and projected to Beaver and Soda Springs. An engraving of the "State Capitol of California, at Sacramento" in the lower left corner.

BYU.

134. <u>1875</u>

Watson's New County Railroad and Distance Map of Wyoming, Utah and Colorado. Entered . . . 1875 by Gaylord Watson.

33 x 41 cm. colored, 1:2,534,400 or 40 miles to 1 inch.

A large Preuss Lake is in Millard County, and Utah Southern Railroad is shown going as far south as Beaver.

Phillips p948.

BYU, LC.

135. <u>1875</u>

Bird's-eye view of Brigham City and Great Salt Lake, Utah Ty. 1875. Drawn and published by E. S. Glover, Salt Lake City. Strobridge & Co. Lith., Cincinnati, Ohio. Entered . . . 1875 by E. S. Glover.

41 x 57 cm.

Oblique aerial view from the mountains northeast of Brigham City. Thirty points of interest are numbered and listed. Brigham City streets are named.

Hebert 923.

UHS, LC.

136. <u>1875</u>

The City of Corinne, Utah, and the Bear River Valley, looking north. Strobridge & Co. Lith. Cincinnati, O.

36 x 54 cm.

Oblique aerial view from the south-southeast. Corinne streets are named. Thirty-three points of interest are numbered and listed.

Published with pamphlet <u>Corinne and Bear River Valley</u>, <u>Utah Territory . . .</u> by E. S. Glover.

UU.

137. <u>1875</u>

Bird's eye view of Logan City, Utah Territory. 1875. Altitude, 4600 feet. Drawn and Published by E. S. Glover. Salt Lake City. A. L. Bancroft & Co. Lith. S. F.

37 x 54 cm.

Oblique aerial view from the west-southwest. Twenty-six points of interest are numbered and listed. Insets of "Mormon Tabernacle" in the lower left and "Zions Cooperative Mercantile Institution" in the lower right.

USU, UHS, UU, BYU.

138. <u>1875</u>

Bird's Eye View of Ogden City, Utah Ty. 1875.
Drawn and published by E. S. Glover, Salt Lake City, Utah Ty.
Strobridge & Co. Lith. Cincinnati, O. Entered . . . 1874 by E. S.
Glover.

35 x 54 cm.

Oblique aerial view from the southwest. Thirty-five points
of interest are named and listed.

Hebert 924.

UHS, LC, BYU.

139. <u>1875</u>

Salt Lake City 1875 by E. S. Glover, printed by Strobridge
& Co. Cincinnati.

62 x 83 cm.

Hebert 929.

LC.

140. <u>1876</u>

Territory of Utah. Compiled from the official records of
the General Land Office and other sources by C. Roeser. Photo lith.
& print by Julius Bien. 16 & 18 Park Place N.Y.

62 x 79 cm. colored, 1:760,320 or 12 miles to 1 inch.

Shows townships, standard parallels, railroad land grant
limits, military and Indian reservations. Railroads are shown completed to Franklin, E. T. City, Alta, Coalville, York, and up
American Fork Canyon. Detail in Uintah and Henry Mountains reflects
Powell's explorations.

Published in Geographical and Political Atlas of the United
States of America in which the Public Land Surveys are now in
operation. S. S. Burdett, Commissioner. Washington City. 1876.
Julius Bien, photolith. & print.

Phillips 1396; Hargett 788; Phillips p948, p926.

WCL, LDSH, UU, LC, GSL, SLP, UHS, BYU.

141. 1876

U.S. Geographical Surveys West of the One-Hundredth Meridian.
Portions of Western Utah & Eastern Nevada. Restored Outline of Lake
Bonneville. Geological data by G. K. Gilbert & E. E. Howell.
Expeditions of 1869, 1871, 1872, & 1873 Under the Command of 1st
Lieut. Geo. M. Wheeler, Corps of Engineers, U.S. Army. By Order of
the Honorable the Secretary of War. Under the Direction of Brig. Gen.
A. A. Humphreys, Chief of Engineers, U.S. Army. J. Bien lith.

48 x 38 cm. colored, 1:1,080,000.

Relief shown by hill shading, modern bodies of water in dark
blue with Lake Bonneville in light blue. Shows from $37^{\circ}30'$ N. to
42° N. and from $111^{\circ}45'$ W. to $115^{\circ}15'$ W.

Described in Wheeler's Geographical Report, pp. 318-320, and
Schmeckebier's Catalogue, page 65.

Phillips 1281, #161.

BYU, UU, USU, LDSH, LC.

142. 1876

Utah. Rand McNally and Company. Chicago. 1876.

30 x 22 cm.

Shows roads, mining districts, railroads completed to Stockton, Bingham Cañon, Alta, Forrest City, York, and proposed to Fillmore and St. George by two different routes. Much information from Froiseth.

Published in Rand McNally & Co.'s Business Atlas, containing large scale maps of each state and territory of the Great Mississippi Valley and Pacific Slope . . . Chicago, Rand, McNally & Co., 1876-77.

Phillips 1397; Phillips p928.

BL, BYU, SLP, UU, USU, LC.

143. 1876

Colton's Wyoming, Colorado and Utah. Published by G. W. and C. B. Colton & Co. No. 172 William St. New York, 1876.

41 x 61 cm colored, 1:2,090,880.

Colored by counties. Shows railroads completed and projected and township lines.

Phillips p948.

LC, SLP, BYU.

144. 1876

Green River Basin.

69 x 106 cm. colored, 1:253,440 or "Scale: Four Miles to one Inch."

Shows area from $40^{\circ}15'$ N. to $41^{\circ}50'$ N. and from $107^{\circ}35'$ W. to $110^{\circ}40'$ W. Surveyed in 1868-69. Shows roads, trails, railroads, and spot elevations. Relief shown by hill shading. Another copy colored to show geology with two geologic profiles along the bottom. Another copy has relief shown by contours, contour interval 300 feet.

Geological and Topographical Atlas Accompanying the Report of the Geological Exploration of the Fortieth Parallel. Made by Authority of the Honorable Secretary of War Under the Direction of Brig. and Brvt. Major General A. A. Humphreys, Chief of Engineers U.S.A. by Clarence King. U.S. Geologist in Charge. 1876. Julius Bien Lith. Map II. Superintendent of Documents # W7.10:18.

Wheat 1270; Phillips 1280.

BYU, LC.

145. 1876

Utah Basin.

69 x 106 cm. colored, 1:253,440 or "Scale: Four Miles to one Inch."

Shows area from $40^{\circ}15'$ N. to $41^{\circ}45'$ N. and from $110^{\circ}45'$ W. to $113^{\circ}50'$ W. Surveyed in 1868-69. Shows roads, trails, spot elevations and railroads to Forest City, Graniteville, Provo, Bingham City, and Logan. Relief shown by hill shading on one copy and by contours on another with the contour interval 300 feet. Another copy colored to show geology with two geologic profiles along the bottom. Heber City is named on the geologic edition but not on the topographic edition.

Geological and Topographical Atlas . . . by Clarence King. 1876. Map III.

Wheat 1270; Phillips 1280.

UHS, BYU, LC.

146. <u>1876</u>

U.S. Geographical Surveys West of the 100th Meridian. Parts of Eastern Nevada and Western Utah, Atlas Sheet No. 49. Expeditions of 1869 and 1872 Under the Command of 1st Lieut. Geo. M. Wheeler, Corps of Engineers, U.S. Army. By Order of the Honorable Wm. M. Belknap, Secretary of War. Under the Direction of Brig. Gen. A. A. Humphreys, Chief of Engineers, U.S. Army. Wyess, Herman & Lang Del.

37 x 48 cm. colored, "Scale 1 inch to 8 miles or 1:506,880." Shows from $39^{\circ}1'$ N. to $40^{\circ}40'$ N. and from $113^{\circ}45'$ W. to $116^{\circ}30'$ W. Shows roads, trails, railroads, and telegraph lines with mileage.

Issued in one hachured andone shaded relief edition.

Described in Schmeckebier's <u>Catalogue</u>, pages 60-65, and Wheeler's <u>Geographical Report</u>, pages 249-252.

LDSH, BYU, UU, LC.

147. <u>1877</u>

Topographical Sketch Showing Observatory Site and Surroundings at Ogden, Utah. Prepared Under the Direction of 1st Lieut. Geo. M. Wheeler; Corps of Engs. U.S. Army. Surveyed by Thompson & Weyss. Weyss & Lang Del. The Graphic Co. N.Y.

16 x 22 cm., 1:17,750.

Shows fields, lots, bhildings, and streets with names.

<u>Report upon United States Geographical Surveys west of the One Hundredth Meridian. Vol. II. Astronomy and Barometric Hypsometry.</u>

Plate No. 2. Washington, G. P. O., 1877. Superintendent of
Documents #W8.5:v.2.

LC, UU, USU, BYU.

148. 1878

County Map of Utah and Nevada. Drawn and Engraved by by
(sic) W. H. Gamble, Philadelphia.

26 x 32 cm. colored, 1:3,000,000.

Shows Rio Virgin county and a large Preuss Lake, now entirely
in Nevada. Juab County is small and there are no towns in the Tintic
district.

Mitchell's New General Atlas. Philadelphia, S. Augustus
Mitchell, 1878, page 91.

BYU.

149. 1878

U.S.-Geographical Surveys West of the 100th Meridian.
Land Classification Map of North-eastern Utah and South-eastern Idaho.
Atlas Sheet No. 41(B). Expeditions of 1877 Under the Command of 1st
Lieut. Geo. M. Wheeler, Corps of Engineers, U.S. Army. By Order of
the Honorable the Secretary of War Under the Direction of Brig. Gen.
A. A. Humphreys, Chief of Engineers, U.S. Army. Weyss, Lang and
Herman Del. Issued June 30, 1878.

36 x 47 cm. colored, "Scale 1 inch to 4 miles or 1:253,440."

Shows area from $41^{\circ}30'$ N. to $42^{\circ}20'$ N. and from 111° W. to
$112^{\circ}22'30"$ W. Shows roads, trails, railroads, and telegraph lines
with mileage.

Issued in one hachure and one land classification edition.

Described in Wheeler's Geographical Report, pages 241-243,
and Schmeckebier's Catalogue, pages 60-65.

GSL, LDSH, UU, BYU, LC.

150. 1878

Froiseth's New Sectional and Mineral Map of Utah. Compiled
from the latest U.S. Government Surveys and other authentic sources.
Exhibiting the Sections, Fractional Sections, Counties, Cities, Towns,
Settlements, Mining Districts, Railroads, and other Internal Improvements. Published by B. A. M. Froiseth. Salt Lake City. 1878.
Second edition thoroughly revised. Re-engraved and brought down to
date. A. L. Bancroft & Co. S.F.

111 x 83 cm. colored, 1:506,880 or "Scale of 8 miles to an
inch."

Shows roads, townships, sections, Indian reservations, mining
districts, and explorers' trails. Railroads are shown completed to
Payson, Stockton, Bingham, Forrest City, Alta, Franklin, and projected
across the Uintah Basin and to St. George by two routes. Bullion
City is the seat of Piute County. In San Juan County is a scroll with
references and population data.

WCL, UU, UHS, BYU.

151. 1878

Rand McNally & Co.'s Utah.

31 x 23 cm. colored, 1:2,000,000.

Toquerville is the seat of Kane County. Bullionville is the
seat of Piute County.

Rand, McNally & Co.'s Business Atlas. Chicago, Rand,
McNally & Co., 1878-1879, page 202.

Phillips 1402.

BYU, LC.

151. 1878

Map of Utah Territory representing the extent of the irrigable,
timber, and pasture lands. Compiled and drawn by Charles Mahon,
J. H. Renshawe, W. H. Graves, and H. Linderkohl for the Commissioner
of Public Lands 1878. Department of the Interior. U.S. Geographical and Geological Survey of the Rocky Mountain Region, J. W.
Powell in charge.

89 x 78 cm. colored, 1:633,600 or 10 miles to 1 inch.

Detailed relief, except that the area southeast of the
Colorado River is blank. The legend distinguishes between railroads,
wagon roads, trails, and telegraph lines. Irrigable lands colored
green, standing timber colored blue, areas destitute of timber on
account of fires colored brown.

In Report on the Lands of the Arid Region of the United
States with a more detailed account of the land of Utah with maps, by
J. W. Powell. Washington, 1878. 45th Cong. 2nd Sess. House Ex.
Doc. 73. Serial 1805, Superintendent of Documents #I17.2:Ar4.

Wheat 1290; Phillips p949.

LDSH, UU, LC, WCL, SLP, UHS, BYU.

152. 1879

Map of the Territory of the United States, West of the
Mississippi River. Prepared by authority of the Hon. the Secretary

of War in the Office of the Chief of Engineers under the direction of
Brig. General A. A. Humphreys chief of Engineers and Brevet Maj.
Gen. U.S. Army. By Edward Freyhold 1879.

259 x 167 cm.

Great detail with many roads. Inset of "Territory of Alaska."
Update of the Warren map of 1857 and the Freyhold map of 1868.

Wheat 1295.

153. 1879

Progress of the Transcontinental Triangulation and Reconnaissance eastward from the Pacific Coast. J. Bien. Photo. lith.
N.Y. Coast and Geodetic Survey Report 1879 No. 30.

26 x 94 cm., ca. 1:2,000,000

Triangulation points in Utah are Mt. Nebo, Beaver Mtn.,
Gosi Ute, and Pioche, Nevada, all sighted on Jeff Davis (Wheeler Peak).

BYU.

154. 1879

Froiseth's New Sectional & Mineral Map of Utah. Compiled from
the latest U.S. Government Surveys and other authentic sources.
Exhibiting the Sections, Fractional Sections, Counties, Cities, Towns,
Settlements, Mining Districts, Railroads, and other Internal Improvements. Published by B. A. M. Froiseth, Salt Lake City, 1879.
A. L. Bancroft & Co. Lith. S. F. Second edition thoroughly
revised. Re-engraved and brought down to date.

111 x 83 cm. colored, "Scale of 8 miles to 1 inch, 1:506,880."

Scroll with population figures and legend in San Juan
County. Boundaries and names of San Juan, Emery, and Uintah Counties,

created in 1880, drawn in red over counties drawn and colored according to 1879 lines. Does not show Silver Reef. Railroads are shown completed to San Francisco Sta. (Frisco), Alta City, Forrest City, Bingham City, Stockton, Coalville, and Franklin. The ten and twenty mile railroad land grant limits are shown. The proposed Denver Pacific Railroad is shown through the Uintah Basin and up the White River. The proposed San Pete and Sevier Railroad is shown from Spanish Fork to the iron mines by way of Thistle, Panguitch, and Parowan with a spur to Bullion City. The Proposed Western Utah Railroad is shown from the site of Milford to St. George.

Another copy dated 1884 in the LDSH shelf list.

BYU.

155. <u>1879</u>

Territory of Utah. Compiled from the official records of the General Land Office and other sources by C. Roeser. Photo Lith. & print by Julius Bien. 16 & 18 Park Place N.Y.

74 x 56 cm. colored, 1:950,400 or "15 miles to 1 inch."

Shows roads, railroads, townships, military and Indian reservations.

Phillips p949; Phillips 1405.

BL, LC, BYU.

156. <u>1879</u>

County map of Utah and Nevada. Drawn and Engraved by by (sic) W. H. Gamble Philadelphia. Entered . . . 1879 by S. Augustus Mitchell.

26 x 33 cm. colored, 1:3,000,000.

Similar to the 1872 and 1878 editions. Colored by counties including Rio Virgin County. A separately colored county is shown north of the Uintahs, but not named. The course of the Colorado River and a large Preuss Lake indicated. Powell's and Wheeler's data were not used. Shows roads and railroads to Payson, Coalville, and Franklin. No settlements are shown in the Sevier Valley south of Ft. Gunnison and no Kanab. Arizona and New Mexico are on the verso.

Colton's General Atlas. New York, G. W. & C. B. Colton, 1879, page 91.

Phillips 4351.

LDSH, LC.

157. 1879

Cram's Railroad & Township Map of Utah published by Geo. F. Cram, proprietor of the western Map Depot. 66 Lake St. Chicago, Ill. 1879.

49 x 41 cm. colored, 1:1,203,840 or 19 miles to 1 inch.

List of towns with population is down the left side. Southern boundary of Summit County extends along Salt Lake base line to Colorado, rather than along the Uintah Mountains watershed.

Phillips p949.

BYU, LC, SLP, UHS, GSL.

158. 1879

Map of the District of the Plateaus of Utah. Triangulation by A. H. Thompson. Topographers J. H. Renshawe, W. H. Graves.

96 x 73 cm. on two sheets, colored, 1:253,440 or "Scale 1 inch = 4 miles."

Relief is shown by contours with the contour interval 250 feet. Shows south central Utah from 37°05' N. to 39°15' N. and from 111°15' W. to 113°20' W. Another sheet colored to show geology. A publication of Powell's Geographical and Geological Survey of the Rocky Mountain Region.

Topographical and Geological Atlas of the District of the High Plateaus of Utah to Accompany the Report of Capt. C. E. Dutton. U.S. Ordinance Corps, Assistant Geologist. Julius Bien Lith. New York. 1879. Atlas Sheet No. 1 (topographic). Atlas Sheet No. 2 (geologic). Superintendent of Documents #I17.2:Ut1.

Phillips 2591; Wheat 1297; Schmeckebier p42; Phillips 2591. UHS, BYU, LC.

159. 1879

Relief map of the District of the High Plateaus of Utah.

55 x 51 cm. colored, 1:316,800 or "Scale 5 miles = 1 inch."

Relief shown by sepia hill shading made to look like a plaster model after the Egloffstein method.

Topographical and Geological Atlas of the District of the High Plateaus of Utah . . . by C. E. Dutton, Atlas Sheet No. 3.

UHS, BYU, LC.

160. 1879

Map of Portions of Utah and Arizona Showing the Arrangement of Faults and Flexures in the Kiababs and High Plateaus.

72 x 50 cm. colored, 1:633,600 or "Scale 1 inch = 10 miles."

Relief shown by hachures with fault lines drawn in. Shows south central Utah and north central Arizona from 35°40' N. to 39°45' N. and from 111°40' W. to 114°05' W.

Topographic and Geologic Atlas of the District of the High Plateaus of Utah . . . by C. E. Dutton, Atlas Sheet No. 4.

UHS, BYU, LC.

161. 1879

Map of Utah Territory. Compiled and drawn by Charles Mahon, J. H. Renshawe, W. H. Graves, and H. Lindenkohl.

91 x 72 cm. colored, 1:633,600.

Shows roads, railroads, cities, and towns. Relief shown in detail except for the area southeast of the Colorado River and south of the La Sal Mountains.

Topographic and Geologic Atlas of the District of the High Plateaus of Utah . . . by C. E. Dutton, Atlas Sheet No. 8.

UHS, BYU, LC.

Chapter VI
1880 - 1889

162. <u>1880</u>

U.S. Geographical Surveys West of the 100th Meridian. Parts
of Southern Idaho & Northeastern Utah, Atlas Sheet No. 41 (A). Expedi-
tion of 1877 Under the Command of 1st Lieut. Geo. M. Wheeler, Corps of
Engineers, U.S. Army. By Order of the Honorable the Secretary of War.
Under the Direction of Brig. Gen. H. G. Wright, Chief of Engineers, U.S.
Army. Weyss, Lang & Herman Del. Issued June 30, 1880.

38 x 47 cm. colored, "Scale 1 inch to 4 miles or 1:253,440."

Shows from 41°31' N. to 42°20' N. and from 112°22'30" W. to
113°45' W. Surveyed in 1877. Shows roads, trails, railroads, and
telegraph lines with mileage.

Issued in one hachured and one land classification edition.

Described in Wheeler's <u>Geographical Report</u>, pages 241-243
and Schmeckebier's <u>Catalogue</u>, pages 60-65.

WCL, UHS, BYU, LC.

163. <u>1880</u>

Rand, McNally & Co.'s Utah.

31 x 23 cm. colored, 1:2,000,000.

Bullionville is the seat of Piute County and Toquerville is the seat of Kane County. No Uintah, San Juan or Emery Counties are shown. Railroads are shown to Fillmore, Black Rock, Alta, Park City, Mt. Pleasant, and up American Fork Canyon.

Rand, McNally & Co.'s Business Atlas. Chicago, Rand McNally & Co. 1880, page 174.

Phillips 1406.

BYU, LC, SUS.

164. 1880

County and Township Map of Utah and Nevada. Entered . . . 1880 by S. Augustus Mitchell.

36 x 55 cm. colored, 1:1,775,000.

Colored by counties with Uintah, Emery, and San Juan counties not shown. Shows roads, township lines, and railroads to Juab, Stockton, Alta, Bingham, and projected to Frisco. Looks like the 1879 General Land Office map.

Mitchell's New General Atlas. Philadelphia, Bradley & Co. page 91.

SLP, SUS.

165. 1881

Utah. Rand, McNally & Co. Engr's. Chicago.

47 x 31 cm. colored, 1:1,400,000.

Colored by counties. County lines current to 1880. Shows roads, township lines, parallels, and railroads to Frisco, Gooseberry Valley (Schofield), Alta, Bingham, and up American Fork Canyon.

Rand, McNally & Co.'s Indexed Atlas of the World. Chicago,
Rand McNally & Co., 1881, pages 744-745.

Phillips 898.

UU, BYU, LC.

166. 1881

County and Township Map of Utah and Nevada. Entered . . . 1881
by S. Augustus Mitchell.

35 x 55 cm. colored, 1:775,000.

Colored by counties. Similar to the 1880 edition, except
the Denver and Rio Grande Western Railroad is projected into Colorado.
Nephi is called "Salt Creek."

Mitchell's New General Atlas. Philadelphia, Bradley & Co.,
1881, page 31.

Phillips 895.

UHS, BYU, LC.

167. 1881

New Railroad and County Map of Utah.

29 x 22 cm colored, 1:2,280,960 or "Scale 36 miles to 1 inch."

Colored by counties. Shows towns, railroads and township
lines.

BYU.

168. 1881

Utah. Rand, McNally & Co.'s Utah.

48 x 32 cm. colored, 1:1,425,000.

Colored by counties.

<u>Rand, McNally & Co.'s New Indexed Business Atlas and Shipper's</u>
<u>Guide</u> . . . Chicago, Rand McNally & Co., 1881, pages 326-327.

Phillips 1408.

BYU, LC.

169. <u>1881</u>

County Map of Utah and Colorado. Copyright by Bradley & Co.
1881.

20 x 28 cm. colored, 1:4,100,000.

Colored by counties. Railroads shown completed to Frisco,
Wales, Stockton, American Fork Canyon, Bingham, Alta, and Park City.

LDSH.

170. <u>1881</u>

Geologic map of the western part of the plateau province.
United States Geological Survey. The Grand Cañon District Atlas.
Sheet II. J. H. Renshawe, Del. Julius Bien & Co. Lith. Geology
by C. E. Dutton, Geologist in Charge.

73 x 45 cm. colored, 1:1,000,000.

Relief shown by hachures and form lines. Utah is shown north
to Salt Lake. Geologic features of the Utah plateau region colored.

<u>Atlas to Accompany the monograph on the Tertiary History of</u>
<u>the Grand Cañon District</u>. 1881. Sheet II. 48th Cong. 2nd Sess.
House Misc. Doc. 35. Serial 2321. Superintendent of Documents
#I19.9:2.

Phillips 1471.

BYU, WCL, UU, LC, SUS.

171. <u>1881</u>

Sketch map of the western part of the plateau province showing the faults of the Grand Cañon District and High Plateaus. Scale about 1:1,000,000. United States Geological Survey. The Grand Cañon District Atlas Sheet III. Julius Bien & Co. lith. N.Y. C. E. Dutton, Geologist in Charge.

73 x 45 cm. colored, 1:1,000,000.

Same map as Sheet II above with fault lines drawn in over the relief.

BYU, WCL, UU, LC, SUS.

172. <u>1881</u>

Geologic Map Showing the South-Western portion of the Mesozoic Terraces and the vicinity of the Hurricane Fault. United States Geological Survey. The Grand Cañon District Atlas Sheet XX. Julius Bien & Co. lith. Geology by C. E. Dutton.

46 x 71 cm. colored, 1:250,000.

Relief shown by contours or form lines. Shows area from 37° N. to 38° N. and from 113° W. to 115° W. The Hurricane Cliff area is colored to show geology.

BYU, LC, UU, WCL, SUS.

173. <u>1881</u>

Geologic Map of the Mesozoic Terraces of the Grand Cañon District and the southern portions of the High Plateaus. United States Geological Survey. The Grand Cañon District Atlas Sheet XXI. Julius Bien & Co. lith. Geology by C. E. Dutton.

46 x 71 cm. colored, 1:250,000.

Shows from 37° N. to 38° N. and from 113° W. to 115° W.
Relief is shown by form lines or contours. Colored to show geology.

BYU, UU, WCL, LC, SUS.

174. 1882

Gray's New Map of Utah. By Frank A. Gray.

38 x 30 cm. colored, "Natural Scale 1:1,584,000."

Colored by counties. No Garfield County is shown. Railroads
are shown completed to Frisco, Tintic, Stockton, Wales, American Fork
Canyon, and past Alta to Park City and Echo. Proposed Rio Grande
Western is on the south side of the Colorado River.

The National Atlas. Philadelphia, O. W. Gray & Son, 1882,
page 153.

Phillips 904.

LDSH, BYU, LC.

175. 1882

Utah. Rand, McNally & Company's Indexed Atlas of the World.
Rand, McNally & Co. Engr's. Chicago.

48 x 32 cm. colored, 1:1,425,000.

Colored by counties.

Rand, McNally & Co.'s Indexed Atlas of the World. Chicago,
Rand, McNally, 1882, pages 744-745.

Phillips 908.

BYU, LC.

176. <u>1883</u>

Cram's Railroad & Township Map of Utah. Published by Geo. F. Cram. Proprietor of the Western Map Depot, 262-264 Wabash Ave., Chicago, Ills. 1883. Entered . . . 1879 by G. F. Cram.

49 x 38 cm. colored, 1:1,203,840 or "Scale 19 miles to 1 inch."

Colored by counties. Railroads shown going to Frisco, Tintic, and from Parley's Park over to Alta. Uintah, San Juan, and Emery counties shown but not Garfield. Nephi is called "Salt Creek."

Pages 184-185 of a Cram atlas.

LDSH, BYU.

177. <u>1883</u>

Utah. Geo. F. Cram Engraver and Publisher. Chicago Ill.

30 x 23 cm. colored, 1:3,400,000.

Colored by counties. Uintah County borders on San Juan County.

<u>Cram's Unrivaled Family Atlas of the World</u>. Chicago, Cram, 1883, page 81.

BYU.

178. <u>1883</u>

Rand McNally & Co's. Utah. Rand McNally & Co. Engr's, Chicago.

47 x 32 cm. colored, 1:1,400,000.

Colored by counties. Garfield County is not shown. Railroads shown to Frisco, Marysville, and to Colorado, but not shown up American Fork Canyon.

BYU.

179. <u>1883</u>

Rand, McNally & Co.'s Indexed County and Township Map of
Utah. Chicago. Rand, McNally & Co.

Phillips p949.

LC.

180. <u>1883</u>

Utah. Rand, McNally & Co. Engr's. Chicago.

48 x 32 cm. colored, 1:1,400,000.

Colored by counties, county boundaries as of 1881. Shows
roads, townships, with railraods shown completed to Frisco, Scofield,
and into Colorado.

<u>Rand, McNally & Co.'s Business Atlas</u>. Chicago, Rand, McNally,
1883, pages 442-443.

SLP.

181. <u>1883</u>

Post Route Map of the Territory of Utah with parts of adjacent
states. U.S. Post Office Dept. Washington, 1883.

101 x 72 cm.

Shows post offices, mail routes and frequency of delivery.

LC.

182. <u>1884</u>

County and Township Map of Utah and Nevada. Copyright by
Wm. M. Bradley & Bro. 1884.

37 x 57 cm. colored.

Colored by counties. Similar to General Land Office maps.
Railroads shown completed to Juab, Moroni, Stockton, Bingham, and up
American Fork Canyon, and proposed to Frisco, Scofield, Tintic, and
to Colorado. Inset of southern Nevada is in the lower left.

In Bradley's Atlas of the World. Philadelphia, W. M. Bradley,
1885, page 56. Another copy paged 90-91.

Phillips 923.

BYU, UU, UHS, LDSH, LC.

183. 1884

Utah Geo. F. Cram engraver and publisher, Chicago Ill.

30 x 23 cm. colored, 1:2,300,000.

Colored by counties. Uintah County borders San Juan County.
Railroad up American Fork Canyon is shown.

The Peoples' Illustrated & Descriptive Family Atlas of the
World. Chicago, Peoples Publishing Co., 1884, page 69.

Phillips 6220.

Cram's Unrivaled Family Atlas of the World. Chicago,
Geo. L. Cram, 1883, page 73.

BYU, LC.

184. 1884

Utah. Copyright 1884 by Rand, McNally & Co., Map Publishers,
Chicago. Rand, McNally & Co. Engr's., Chicago.

47 x 32 cm. colored, 1:1,425,000.

Colored by counties. Shows roads, railroads, and township
lines. The information is current.

GSL, SLP, UU, UHS.

185. <u>1884</u>

Territory of Utah. Compiled from the official records of the General Land Office and other sources under supervision of G.P. Strum, Principal Draughtsman GLO. Photo lith. & print by Julius Bien & Co. 139 Duane St. N.Y. Compiled by A. F. Dinsmore. Drawn by W. Naylor & G. P. Strum.

66 x 51 cm. colored, 1:950,400 or "Scale 15 Miles to 1 Inch."

Shows townships, roads, railroads, military and Indian reservations, and land grant limits of the Central Pacific and Union Pacific. The southeastern quarter is fairly empty.

Hargett 789.

BYU, UHS, LDSH, LC.

186, <u>1884</u>

Brigham City, Box Elder Co., Utah. Mar. 1884. Sanborn Map Company, New York.

4 sheets, 64 x 54 cm. colored, 1:600 or 50 feet to 1 inch.

Shows from Fanning St. to Box Elder St. and from N. Wall St. to Tabernacle St., plus Brigham City Woolen Mills and Brigham City Flouring Mill Co.

UU, LC.

187. <u>1884</u>

Corrine, Box Elder Co., Utah. Feb. 1884. Sanborn Map Company, New York.

2 sheets, 64 x 54 cm. colored, 1:600.

LC.

188. <u>1884</u>

Ogden, Weber Co., Utah. Jan. 1884. Sanborn Map Company,
New York.

17 sheets, 64 x 54 cm. colored, 1:600.

Shows from Wall to Spring and from Second to Seventh;
plus Phoenix Mills, Grove Brewery, Ogden City Brewery, Ogden Flour
Mill, Ogden Woolen Mills, Utah Vinegar Works, and the area around the
railroad depot.

UU, LC.

189. <u>1884</u>

Salt Lake City, Salt Lake Co., Utah. Jan. 1884. Sanborn
Map Company, New York.

17 sheets, 64 x 54 cm. colored, 1:600.

Shows from First West to Second East and from North Temple
to Fourth South.

UU, LC.

190. <u>1885</u>

Logan, Cache Co., Utah. Jan. 1885. Sanborn Map Company,
New York.

5 sheets, 64 x 54 cm. colored, 1:600.

Shows from Fourth to First and from Franklin to Johnson,
plus the United Order Manufacturing & Building Co. and the area
around the Northern Utah Railroad depot on West and Walnut.

UU, LC.

191. <u>1885</u>

Railroad & Township Map of Utah. Entered . . . 1879 . . .

49 x 38 cm. colored, 1:1,203,840 or "Scale 19 miles to 1 inch."

Colored by counties. Though dated 1879 much information indicates an 1885 publication. Garfield County is named but the western border is not colored. Bullion City is the seat of Piute County. A railroad is shown from Parley's Park over the mountains to Alta, also up American Fork Canyon, and to Colorado, Scofield, Tintic, and Frisco.

Paged 194-195.

BYU.

192. <u>1885</u>

Salt Lake City, prepared expressly for Crofutt's Salt Lake City Directory 1885. Platted and Drawn by B. A. M. Froiseth, C. E. Salt Lake City, Utah. Hilpert & Chandler, engravers, Chicago. . . . entered 1885 by A. M. Crofutt.

42 x 55 cm., "Scale: 96 rods to 1 inch."

Shows townships, sections, wards, streets, canals, and references to thirty-four important buildings. Shows plans for buildings at Ft. Douglas. Dr. Young's Private Asylum is in the lower right corner.

BYU, LDSH.

193. <u>1885</u>

West's New Sectional & Topographical Map of Utah. Containing all Government Land & Topographical Surveys to date. Sections, Fractional Sections, Townships, Ranges, Counties, Cities, Towns,

Mining Districts, Wagon Roads. Railways and numerous other Internal
Improvements. Prepared and published under the authority of the
Legislative Assembly of the Territory of Utah by Joseph A. West.
C. E. 1885.

69 x 44 cm., 1:1,013,760 or "Scale 16 miles to 1 inch."

A scroll with information is in San Juan County. Plans are
along the bottom of Manti City, Nephi City, Provo City, Salt Lake
City, Ogden City, Logan City, and Coalville. Shows townships,
sections, roads, railroads, and mining districts. Detailed relief
shown by hachures.

Another issue is 137 x 90 cm., 1:506,880 or 8 miles to 1 inch.
Another issue is 120 x 182 cm., 1:380,160 or 6 miles to 1 inch.

Phillips p949.

USU, LDSH, UHS, GSL, SLP, BYU, LC.

194. <u>1885</u>

Utah-Col. Ashley Sheet. U.S. Geological Survey. Triangulation and Topography by the King and Powell Surveys. Edition of
Dec. 1885.

45 x 34 cm. colored, 1:250,000.

Relief shown by contours, contour interval 250 feet.
Shows from 40° N. to 41° N. and from 109° W. to 110° W. Ashley is
now Vernal. Surveyed in 1885.

USU, UHS, LDSH, BYU, LC.

195. <u>1885</u>

Utah Beaver Sheet. U.S. Geological Survey. Triangulation and
Topography by the Powell and Wheeler Surveys. Edition of July 1885.

45 x 35 cm. colored, 1:250,000.

Relief shown by contours, contour interval 250 feet.
Shows from 38° N. to 39° N. and from 112° W. to 113° W. Surveyed in
1885. Reprinted in 1899.

USU, UHS, LDSH, BYU, LC.

196. <u>1885</u>

Utah East Tavaputs Sheet. U.S. Geological Survey.
Triangulation by the Hayden and Powell Surveys. Edition of Dec. 1885.

45 x 35 cm. colored, 1:250,000.

Relief shown by contours, contour interval 250 feet.
Shows from 39° N. to 40° N. and from 109° W. to 110° W. Surveyed in
1877. Reprinted in 1896.

USU, UHS, LDSH, BYU, LC.

197. <u>1885</u>

Utah La Sal Sheet. U.S. Geological Survey, Triangulation
and Topography by the Hayden and Powell Surveys. Edition of Dec. 1885.

45 x 35 cm. colored, 1:250,000.

Relief shown by contours, contour interval 250 feet. Shows
from 38° N. to 39° N. and from 109° W. to 110° W. Surveyed in 1877.

USU, UHS, LDSH, BYU, LC.

198. <u>1885</u>

Utah Manti Sheet. U.S. Geological Survey. Triangulation
and Topography by the Powell Survey. Edition of Dec. 1885.

45 x 35 cm. colored, 1:250,000.

Relief shown by contours, contour interval 250 feet. Shows from 39° N. to 40° N. and from 111° W. to 112° W. Surveyed in 1885. Reprinted in 1895.

USU, UHS, LDSH, BYU, LC.

199. <u>1885</u>

Nevada-Utah Pioche Sheet. U.S. Geological Survey. Triangulation and Topography by the Powell and Wheeler Surveys. Edition of Dec. 1885.

45 x 36 cm. colored, 1:250,000.

Relief shown by contours, contour interval 250 feet. Shows from 37° N. to 38° N. and from 114° W. to 115° W. Surveyed in 1884.

LDSH, BYU, LC.

200. <u>1885</u>

Utah Salt Lake Sheet. U.S. Geological Survey. Triangulation and Topography by the King and Powell Surveys. Edition of Oct. 1885.

45 x 34 cm. colored, 1:250,000.

Relief shown by contours, contour interval 250 feet. Shows from 49° N. to 41° N. and from 111° W. to 112° W. Surveyed in 1884.

LDSH, USU, BYU, LC.

201. <u>1885</u>

Utah San Rafael Sheet. U.S. Geological Survey. Triangulation and Topography by the Powell Survey. Edition of Dec. 1885.

45 x 35 cm. colored, 1:250,000.

Relief shown by contours, contour interval 250 feet. Shows from 38° N. to 39° N. and from 110° W. to 111° W. Surveyed in 1884.

LDSH, USU, HUS, BYU, LC.

202. <u>1885</u>

Utah Sevier Desert Sheet. U.S. Geological Survey. Triangulation and Topography by the Wheeler and Powell Surveys. Edition of
Dec. 1885.

45 x 35 cm. colored, 1:250,000.

Relief shown by contours, contour interval 250 feet. Shows
from 39°N to 40°N. and from 112° W. to 113° W. Surveyed in 1879.
Reprinted 1897.

USU, UHS, LDSH, BYU, LC.

203. <u>1885</u>

Utah Tooele Valley Sheet. U.S. Geological Survey. Triangulation and Topography by the King and Wheeler Surveys. Edition of
Dec. 1885.

45 x 34 cm. colored, 1:250,000.

Relief shown by contours, contour interval 250 feet. Shows
from 40° N. to 41° N. and from 112° W. to 113° W. Surveyed in 1884.

USU, UHS, LDSH, BYU, LC.

204. <u>1885</u>

Utah Uintah Sheet. U.S. Geological Survey. Triangulation
and Topography by the King and Powell Surveys. Edition of Dec. 1885.

45 x 34 cm. colored, 1:250,000.

Relief shown by contours, contour interval 250 feet. Shows
40° N. to 41° N. and from 110° W. to 111° W. Surveyed in 1877.
Reprinted in 1897.

USU, UHS, LDSH, BYU, LC.

205. <u>1886</u>

Utah Escalante Sheet. U.S. Geological Survey. Triangulation and Topography by the Powell Survey. Edition of Jan. 1886.

45 x 36 cm. colored, 1:250,000.

Relief shown by contours, contour interval 250 feet. Shows from 37° N. to 38° N. and from 111° W. to 112° W. Surveyed in 1885. Reprinted in 1896.

USU, UHS, LDSH, BYU, LC.

206. <u>1886</u>

Utah Kanab Sheet. U.S. Geological Survey. Triangulation and Topography by the Powell Survey. Edition of Jan. 1886.

45 x 36 cm. colored, 1:250,000.

Shows from 37° N. to 38° N. and from 112° W. to 113° W. Relief shown by contours, contour interval 250 feet. Surveyed in 1879. Reprinted in 1896.

USU, UHS, LDSH, BYU, LC.

207. <u>1886</u>

Utah Price River Sheet. U.S. Geological Survey. Triangulation and Topography by the Powell Survey. Edition of Jan. 1886.

45 x 35 cm. colored, 1:250,000.

Shows from 39° N. to 40° N. and from 110° W. to 111° W. Relief shown by contours, contour interval 250 feet. Surveyed in 1885.

USU, UHS, LDSH, BYU, LC.

208. <u>1886</u>

    Utah and Nevada. Copyright 1886 by Wm. M. Bradley & Bro.

    37 x 57 cm. colored, 1:1,775,000.

    Inset of "Southern Portion of Nevada" is in the lower left.

Shows roads, railroads, and township lines.

    <u>Bradley's Atlas of the World</u>. Philadelphia, Bradley, 1886,

page 56.

    Phillips 6227.

    BYU, LC.

209. <u>1886</u>

    Utah. Engraved for Gaskell's Atlas of the World.

    31 x 24 cm. colored, 1:2,280,000.

    Colored by counties. Shows railroads. Looks like a Rand,

McNally map.

    <u>Gaskell's New and Complete Family Atlas of the World</u>.

Chicago, Fairbanks & Palmer, 1886, page 127.

    Phillips 932.

    LDSH, LC.

210. <u>1886</u>

    Utah. Phillips & Hunt. 805 Broadway. L. B. Folger Sc. Cin.

    29 x 23 cm. colored, 1:2,375,000.

    Nephi is called "Salt Creek." The Railroad up American Fork

Canyon is still shown.

    <u>A. W. H. DuPuy Atlas</u>. New York, Phillips & Hunt, 1886.

    BYU.

211. <u>1887</u>

County and Township Map of Utah and Nevada. Copyright 1887
by Wm. M. Bradley & Bro.

37 x 57 cm. colored.

Colored by counties. Shows township lines. Nevada is copyrighted 1884. Inset of southern Nevada is in lower left.

Paged 90-91.

BYU, SUS.

212. <u>1887</u>

Utah. George F. Cram Company. Chicago, 1887.

29 x 24 cm. colored, 1:2,300,000.

<u>Cram's Unrivaled Atlas of the World</u>. Chicago, H. S.
Stebbens, 1887, page 76.

Phillips 938.

USU, LC.

213. <u>1887</u>

Utah, Rand, McNally & Co. Engr's. Chicago.

48 x 32 cm. colored, 1:1,400,000.

Colored by counties. Shows roads, railroads, and townships.

<u>Rand, McNally & Company's New Indexed Atlas of the World</u>.
Chicago, Rand, McNally, 1887, pages 660-661.

Phillips 6237.

BYU, LC, SUS.

214. <u>1887</u>

Salt Lake City, 1887. Gast.-St. L. & N.Y. Entered . . .
1887, by S. W. Darke & Co. Salt Lake City.

51 x 83 cm.

Oblique aerial view looking north from over 4th South between
West Temple and Main. In lower left is a view of Fort Douglas from
the southwest and an inset of City Hall.

"Salt Lake City Illustrated by Sydney W. Darke" is in the
lower right.

UU.

215. <u>1887</u>

Salt Lake City, Utah. Drawn for the Chamber of Commerce by
Edmund Wilkes, Civil Engineer. 1887. The Denver Litho. Co. Denver,
Colo. Salt Lake City, Lynch & Glassman.

42 x 57 cm.

Phillips p772.

LC.

216. <u>1888</u>

Utah. Rand, McNally & Co. Engr's. Chicago.

48 x 32 cm. colored, 1:1,425,000.

Colored by counties. Shows roads, railroads, and township
lines.

<u>Rand, McNally & Co.'s New Indexed Atlas of the World.</u>
Chicago, Rand, McNally, 1888-9, pages 678-679.

LDSH.

217. <u>1888</u>

    Weber County. Washington Jenks.

    4 sheets, 93 x 64 cm., 1:39,600.

    LC.

218. <u>1888</u>

    Provo, Utah Co., Utah. Feb. 1888. Sanborn Map Company, New York.

    4 sheets, 64 x 54 cm. colored, 1:600.

    Shows from Main St. to K St. and from 8th St. to 6th St., plus Provo M'f'g. Co. Woolen Mills and the area around the Utah Central Railroad depot from I St. to K St.

    UU, LC.

219. <u>1888</u>

    Map of Salt Lake City and vicinity, Utah. Compiled from official records and actual surveys by Browne and Brooks, Feb. 20th, 1888. New York. G. W. & C. B. Colton & Co. 1888.

    125 x 130 cm. colored, 1:12,672 or 5 inches to 1 mile.

    Colored by wards. Shows block numbers, lot numbers, and important buildings.

    Phillips p772.

    Another issue 60 x 71 cm., 1:25,344 or 2½ inches to 1 mile.

    LDSH, BYU, SLP, UHS, LC.

220. <u>1889</u>

    Map of that portion of the Department of the Platte and adjacent territory West of the 103rd Meridian. Projected and compiled

at the Engineer Office, Department of the Platte by First Lieut.
Hiram M. Chittenden, Corps of Eng'rs, U.S.A. assisted by Augustus
Smith, Topographical Assistant, U.S.A. drawn by Augustus Smith,
Topographical Assistant, U.S.A. 1889. Published in the Office of the
Chief of Engineers, U.S.A.

2 sheets, 64 x 107 cm., 1:1,000,000.

List of authorities in lower left and right. Shows Utah,
Colorado, Wyoming, and Southeast Idaho to 114°30' W. Shows roads,
railroads, and reservation boundaries.

UU.

221. <u>1889</u>

Utah. Engraved for Standard Atlas of the World.

30 x 24 cm. colored, 1:2,300,000.

Shows railroads to Frisco, Wales, and up American Fork
Canyon.

<u>The Standard Atlas and Gazetteer of the World</u>. Chicago,
Standard Publishing, 1889, page 161.

BYU.

222. <u>1889</u>

Utah and Nevada. Copyright by Wm. M. Bradley & Bro.

35 x 55 cm. colored, 1:1,650,000.

Railroads shown completed to Frisco, Scofield, American Fork
Canyon, and Colorado.

<u>Bradley's Atlas of the World</u> . . . Philadelphia, W. M.
Bradley & Co., 1893, pages 55-56.

Phillips 980.

BYU, LC.

223. <u>1889</u>

Territory of Utah. Compiled from the official records of the General Land Office and other sources. Photo lith. & print by Julius Bien & Co. 139 Duane St. N.Y. Compiled and drawn by A. F. Dinsmore.

68 x 52 cm. colored, 1:950,400 or 15 miles to 1 inch.

Shows roads, railroads, and settlements. Southeastern Utah filled in except for southern and western San Juan County.

Hargett 790.

LDSH, BYU, USU, LC.

224. <u>1889</u>

Ogden. Eugene F. Darling.

56 x 91 cm.

Hebert 925.

LC.

225. <u>1889</u>

Park City, Summit Co., Utah. Dec. 1889. Sanborn Map Company, New York.

13 sheets, 64 x 54 cm. colored, 1:600.

Shows from Norfolk Ave. to Marsac Ave. and from Crescent to Seventh; plus Park City Sampling Mill, Ontario Silver Mining Co.'s No. 1 and No. 2 Hoisting W'ks., Ontario Quartz Crushing Mill, Ontario Silver Mining Co.'s No. 3 Hoisting Works, Massachusetts

Mining Co. Empire Hoisting W'ks., Union Concentrator, Anchor Mining
Co.'s Intermediate Shaft Compressor House, Comstock Mining Co.'s
Tunnel, Daly Mining Co.'s Hoisting W'ks., Anchor Mining Co.'s
Hoisting W'ks., Silver King Mining Co.'s Hoisting Works, Woodside
Mining Co.'s Hoisting Works, Northland Mining Co.'s Hoisting Works,
May Flower No. 7 Mining Co.'s Hoisting Works, Alliance Mining Co.'s
"Hanhauer Tunnel," Crescent Mining Co.'s Mine, Alliance Mining Co.'s
"Jones Tunnel," and Apex Mining Co.'s Mine.

UU. LC.

226. <u>1889</u>

Salt Lake City, Salt Lake Co., Utah. 1889. Sanborn Map
Company, New York.

63 sheets, 64 x 54 cm. colored, 1:600.

Shows from Fifth West to Sixth East and from First North
to Fifth South; plus Continental Oil Co.'s Storage Depot, Bee Hive
Planning Mill, Burton Gardner Mattress Fac., Lumber-Yard, Fence Fac.,
JeRemy & Co.'s Salt Works, Henry Wagner's Lager Beer Brewery,
A. Fisher Brewing Co.'s Brewery, Salt Lake City Brewing Co.'s
Brewery, Salt Lake Soap Co.'s W'ks., Salt Lake Chemical Works,
Utah Broom Co.'s Fac., Zions Commercial Mercantile Institute Tannery,
J. W. Summerhays and Co.'s Sheep Skin Tannery, The City Mill & Sheep
Skin Tannery, Utah Brewery, Salt Lake Miller and Elevator Co., Salt
Lake Glass W'ks., Utah Soap M'f'g. Co.'s W'ks., Deseret Woolen
Mills Co., Queen of the Valley Roller Mill, Liberty Park Roller Mill
Co.'s Flour Mill, Wasatch Patent Roller Mills, County Infirmary,
Bedis Hot Springs, Holy Cross Hospital.

UU, LC.

227. <u>1889</u>

    Salt Lake City, Utah. Compiled from the records and actual surveys by Simon F. Mackie, Civil Engineer. Published by W. H. Whitney, December 1st, 1889 for Saltair Beach Association. Location of Property 12 Miles due West from Salt Lake City, Utah. Parsons & Derge, Booksellers and Stationers, No. 209 South Main Street, Exclusive Retail Agents for this Map. Entered . . . 1889 by W.H. Whitney. Everts and Howell, Engravers, Philadelphia, Pa.

    51 x 86 cm. colored, 1:22,800.

    Shows blocks, lots, subdivisions, wards, townships, and sections. Two insets shown in upper left: "The Vicinity of Salt Lake City," and "Property of the Saltair Beach Association Located 12 Miles West of Salt Lake City." Colored by subdivisions.

    Phillips p773.

    Another copy does not include the Saltair inset.

    BYU, UU, LDSH, LC.

228. <u>1889</u>

    Though originally issued separately, the maps of Geo. M. Wheeler's United States Geographical Surveys West of the One Hundredth Meridian are often found bound in the following atlases published in 1889:

<u>Geological Atlas Projected to Illustrated Geographical Explorations and Surveys West of the 100th Meridian of Longitude Prosecuted in Accordance with Acts of Congress under the Authority of the Honorable the Secretary of War, and the Direction of Brig.</u>

Gen'l. A. A. Humphreys, Chief of Engineers, U.S. Army. Embracing
Results of the Different Expeditions Under the Command of 1st Lieut.
Geo. M. Wheeler, Corps of Engineers. Julius Bien, lith.

Topographical Atlas Projected to Illustrate United States
Geographical Surveys West of the 100th Meridian of Longitude Prose-
cuted in Accordance with Acts of Congress. Under the Authority of the
Honorable the Secretary of War, and the Direction of Brig. Gen'l. A. A.
Humphreys, Chief of Engineers, U.S. Army. Embracing Results of the
Different Expeditions Under the Command of 1st Lieut. Geo M. Wheeler,
Corps of Engineers. Julius Bien, lith.

Wheat 1250; Phillipa 1281.

Superintendent of Documents #W8.2:G29 and W8.2:T62.

229. 1889

Utah.

26 x 19 cm. colored, 1:3,500,000.

Separate maps of Utah and Arizona on one sheet colored with
surrounding states outlined.

Page 44d of a Scribner atlas, New York, 1889.

BYU, SUS.

Chapter VII
1890 - 1899

230. <u>1890</u>

Map of Lake Bonneville (a water body of the quaternary

period) by G. K. Gilbert, assisted by Gilbert Thompson, Israel

C. Russell, H. A. Wheeler, and Albert L. Webster. Drawn by Gilbert

Thompson and J. H. Renshawe. U.S. Geological Survey Report on Lake

Bonneville. Julius Bien & Co. Lith.

70 x 45 cm. colored, 1:887,040.

Note. "The topographic base was compiled from the published

maps of the Survey of the Fortieth Parallel, and from the published

and unpublished maps of the Survey of the Rocky Mountain Region

and of the U.S. Engineer Surveys West of the 100th Meridian, together

with the field notes of the Survey." Relief shown by hill shading and

contours.

In <u>Lake Bonneville</u>, by Grove Karl Gilbert, Washington,

G. P. O., 1890. U.S. Geological Survey Monographs, Vol. I. Serial

2776. Superintendent of Documents #I19.9:1.

BYU, UHS, UU, USU, SLP, LC.

231. <u>1890</u>

Saltair Beach. 13 Miles due West of Salt Lake City, Utah.

Matthew White proprietor. Surveyed August 1890 by Robert Gorlinski

U.S. Deputy Surveyor & Civil and Mining Engineer. Salt Lake Litho.
Co.

    31 x 33 cm., 1:6,000.

    Shows lots, blocks, and sections with numbers and streets
with names.

    LDSH.

323. 1890

    Map of the Bear River Valley and its system of Irrigation
from the Bear River Canal, Utah Territory. Hudson-Kimberly Pub. Co.
Kansas City.

    52 x 36 cm., 1:152,000.

    Shows railroads, roads, township and section lines.
Shows from T.6N. to T.13N. and from R.1W. to R.5W. Insets of:
(1) Corrine City, or Box Elder County, Territory of Utah, and (2) Map
showing Bear Lake and Bear Rivers. Promotional information on the
verso.

    LDSH.

233. 1890

    Perspective map of Ogden, Utah. 1890. Copyrighted and
published by American Publishing Co. Cor. South Water & Ferry Sts.
Milwaukee, Wis. W. W. Browning & Co. Genl. Agents for Ogden
perspective views.

    51 x 85 cm. colored.

    Oblique aerial view from the west. Some streets are named.
An Inset of the mouth of Ogden Canyon is in the lower left. Nine
insets of prominent buildings are along the top border.

Hebert 926.

UHS, LC.

234. <u>1890</u>

   Salt Lake County.

   2 sheets, 69 x 150 cm., 1:42,000.

   LC.

235. <u>1890</u>

   Map of Salt Lake City and environs, Utah. 1890. Compiled

by Jesse W. Fox, Jr. City Surveyor. Published by W. H. Whitney.

L. H. Everts & Co. Phila. 1890.

   175 x 219 cm., 1:7,920 or "Scale 660 feet to the inch."

   Phillips p773.

   LC.

236. <u>1890</u>

   American Fork, Utah Co., Utah. Sept. 1890. Sanborn Map

Company, New York.

   6 sheets, 64 x 54 cm. colored, 1:600.

   Shows from Union to John and from Adams to South, plus

Starr Roller Mills and American Fork City Roller Mills.

   UU, LC.

237. <u>1890</u>

   Bingham Canyon, Salt Lake Co., Utah. Oct. 1890. Sanborn

Map Company, New York.

   4 sheets, 64 x 54 cm. colored, 1:600.

Shows Main St., plus Winamuck Mining Co.'s Hoisting Works, Bevan Mining & Milling Co.'s Gold Mill, West Mountain Mining Co.'s Concentrator, Bingham Mining & Milling Co.'s Gold Mill, Niagara Mining & Smelting Co.'s Concentrator, South Galena Mining & Milling Co.'s Hoisting Works, South Galena Mining Co.'s Concentrator, Lead Mine Hoisting Works, Brooklyn Mine Hoisting Works, Yosemite No. 2 Hoisting Works, Lead Mine Co.'s Lead Mill, Yosmite No. 1 Hoisting Works.

UU, LC.

238. <u>1890</u>

Brigham City, Box Elder Co., Utah. Nov. 1890. Sanborn Map Company, New York.

7 sheets, 64 x 54 cm. colored, 1:600.

Shows from Fanning St. to Box Elder St. and from North St. to Tabernacle St., plus Brigham City Woolen Mills and Brigham City Flouring Mill Co.'s Box Elder Mill.

UU, LC.

239. <u>1890</u>

Corrine, Box Elder Co., Utah. Nov. 1890. Sanborn Map Company, New York.

3 sheets, 65 x 54 cm. colored, 1:600.

Shows from 8th St. to 2nd St. and from Washington St. to Arizona St., plus Continental Brewery and Corinne Flour Mills.

UU, LC.

240. <u>1890</u>

Eureka, Juab Co., Utah. Nov. 1890. Sanborn Map Company, New York.

4 sheets, 64 x 54 cm. colored, 1:600.

Shows about two blocks on either side of Main St.; plus Centennial Eureka Mining Co.'s Hoisting Works, Bullion Beck and California Mining Co.'s Hoisting Works, Gemini Mining Co.'s Excelsior Hoisting Works, Eureka Hill Mining Co.'s Hoisting Works.

UU, LC.

241. <u>1890</u>

Lehi, Utah Co., Utah. Sept. 1890. Sanborn Map Company, New York.

4 sheets, 64 x 54 cm. colored, 1:600.

Shows from 5th West to 1st East and from 1st North to 1st South, plus Spring Creek Flouring Mill and the area around the Utah Central Railroad depot.

UU, LC.

242. <u>1890</u>

Logan, Cache Co., Utah. Nov. 1890. Sanborn Map Company, New York.

15 sheets, 65 x 54 cm. colored, 1:600.

Shows from Sixth to First South and from D St. to I St., plus the area around the Utah Northern Railroad depot on A St. and B St. and the Agricultural College of Utah.

UU, LC.

243. <u>1890</u>

Nephi, Juab Co. Utah. Sept. 1890. Sanborn Map Company, New York.

7 sheets, 64 x 54 cm. colored, 1:600.

Shows from West to Bryan and from Wormwood to Sutton, plus Nephi Plaster and M'f'g. Co.'s W'ks., Nephi Mill and M'f'g. Co.'s Water Power Roller Mill and the area around the railroad depot.

UU, LC.

244. <u>1890</u>

Ogden, Weber Co., Utah. 1890. Sanborn Map Company, New York.

55 sheets, 65 x 54 cm. colored, 1:600.

Shows from Wall Ave. to Monroe Ave. and from 20th to 29th plus Ogden Milling and Elevator Co.'s Phoenix Roller Mills, Christian Garff's Sash, Door & Blind and Box Fact'y, Utah Canning Co.'s Works, Territorial Reform School, Ogden Woolen Mills, Jos. Jackson Pressed Brick Works, Hot Springs Health Resort, Ogden Military Academy.

UU, UHS (copy corrected to Oct. 1898), LC.

245. <u>1890</u>

Payson, Utah Co., Utah. Sept. 1890. Sanborn Map Company, New York.

5 sheets, 64 x 54 cm. colored, 1:600.

Shows from 14th St. to 7th St. and from B St. to H St.

UU, LC.

246. <u>1890</u>

Pleasant Grove, Utah Co., Utah. Sept. 1890. Sanborn Map Company, New York.

4 sheets, 64 x 54 cm colored, 1:600.

Shows from 4th West St. to Center and from 2nd North St. to 2nd South St., plus Pleasant Grove Roller Mills and the area around the railroad depot.

UU, LC.

247. <u>1890</u>

Provo, Utah Co., Utah. Aug. 1890. Sanborn Map Company, New York.

21 sheets, 64 x 54 cm. colored, 1:600.

Shows from D St. to N St. and from 10th St. to 1st St.; plus Provo Pottery, Excelsior Roller Mills, and Utah Territorial Insane Asylum.

UU, LC.

248. <u>1890</u>

Spanish Fork, Utah Co., Utah. Sept. 1890. Sanborn Map Company, New York.

5 sheets, 64 x 54 cm. colored, 1:600.

Shows from First West to First East and from Fifth North to Fourth South; plus C. R. Larson's Mach. Shop and Foundary, Gem Roller Mills, Spanish Fork Coop Institution.

UU, LC.

249. <u>1890</u>

Springville, Utah Co., Utah. Sept. 1890. Sanborn Map Company, New York.

5 sheets, 64 x 54 cm. colored, 1:600.

Shows from Potter to Haymond and from North to below South, plus Springville Woolen Mills.

UU, LC.

250. <u>1890</u>

Railroad and County Map of Utah. Geo. F. Cram, Engraver and Publisher, Chicago.

55 x 39 cm. colored, 1:1,300,000.

Shows Garfield County but not Grand County. Railroads are shown completed to Frisco, Ephriam, Colorado, and Mud Creek (Winter Quarters).

Pages 232, 233 of a Cram atlas. Richard Fitch dates it 1890.

SUS.

251. <u>1891</u>

Utah.

34 x 26 cm. colored, 1:1,800,000.

Shows Grand County and railroads completed to Marysville, from Ft. Douglas to Red Butte and Wagner, and south from Milford into Nevada.

<u>Unrivaled Atlas of the World</u>. Kansas City, Geo. F. Cram, 1891, page 95. Another copy is page 229 of L. T. Palmer's <u>Standard Atlas</u> with Idaho on the verso.

UU, BYU, LC.

252. <u>1891</u>

The D. W. Ellis Map of Ogden City, Utah Ty. 1891. Compiled from records city engineers office, county records and surveys, etc. Scale 500 ft. = 1 inch. Drawn and compiled by D. W. Ellis. C. E. Cactus Printing Co., Pueblo, Colo.

65 x 43 cm. colored, 1:20,000.

Colored by subdivisions. Shows wards, township and section lines, streets are named, blocks and lots are numbered.

LDSH.

253. <u>1891</u>

Map of Utah. Copyright 1891 by The Matthews-Northrup Co. Complete Engraving Works, Buffalo and New York.

30 x 24 cm. colored, 1:2,027,520 or "32 miles to the inch."

Colored by counties. County boundaries are current. Shows railroads and township lines.

<u>The Library Atlas of Modern Geography</u>, New York, Appleton, 1892, page 99.

Phillips 969.

SLP, BYU, LC.

254. <u>1891</u>

Utah St. George Sheet, U.S. Geological Survey. Triangulation and Topography by the Powell Survey. Edition of July 1890.

45 x 36 cm. colored, 1:250,000.

Relief shown by contours, contour interval 250 feet. Shows from 37° N. to 38° N. and from 113° W. to 114° W. Surveyed in 1885.

Reprinted 1895.

USU, UHS, BYU, LDSH, LC.

255. <u>1891</u>

Salt Lake City 1891 by H. Wellge published by American Pub.
Co. Milwaukee.

61 x 112 cm. colored.

Oblique aerial view from the south-southeast. Built up area
ends at Ninth South. Compliments of the Midland Investment Co. Index
to 59 major sites. Nine insets of Garfield Beach, American National
Bank, Progress Building, Hotel Ontario, Temple grounds, Wasatch Building
and Midland Investment Company's three plats or additions.

Hebert 930.

BYU, LC.

256. <u>1892</u>

[Utah] Atlas of the World. Rand, McNally & Co.'s Family
Atlas Map of Utah. Copyright 1892 by Rand, McNally & Co.

31 x 23 cm. colored, 1:2,400,000.

Colored by counties. Shows railroads to Salina, Scofield,
and Frisco.

<u>Rand, McNally & Co.'s Universal Atlas of the World</u>.
Chicago, Rand, McNally, 1894, page 76.

LDSH.

257. <u>1892</u>

Rand, McNally & Co.'s Utah. Rand, McNally & Co. Engr's.
Chicago. Rand, McNally & Co.'s Business Atlas Map of Utah 1888.

Rand, McNally & Co., Map Publishers and Engravers, Chicago,
1892.

46 x 32 cm. colored, 1:1,400,000.

Colored by counties. County boundaries as of 1890. Wayne
County is not shown. Shows roads, township lines and railroads
completed to Frisco, Maryville, two lines to Tintic, and a projected
line from Milford to Nevada.

Copies variously paged 286, 292, 295, 324.

LDSH, SLP, BYU, SUS.

258. 1892

Utah.

34 x 26 cm. colored, 1:1,800,000.

Indexes to other plates listed down both sides. Shows
township lines.

From various Cram atlases, paged 238, 268, 269.

BYU.

259. 1892

Ephraim, Sanpete Co., Utah. Sept. 1892. Sanborn Map
Company, New York.

2 sheets, 64 x 54 cm. colored, 1:600.

Shows from Main St. to A East and from 2nd North St. to
2nd South St., plus Climax Roller Mills.

UU, LC.

260. <u>1892</u>

Manti, Sanpete Co., Utah. Sept. 1892. Sanborn Map
Company, New York.

6 sheets, 64 x 54 cm. colored, 1:600.

Shows from 3rd West to 1st East and from 4th North to 4th
South, plus Manti Roller Mills.

UU, LC.

261. <u>1892</u>

Mount Pleasant, Sanpete Co., Utah. Aug. 1892. Sanborn Map
Company, New York.

5 sheets, 64 x 54 cm. colored, 1:600.

Shows from 5th West to 2nd East and from 1st North to 3rd
South, plus Mount Pleasant Mill Company.

UU, LC.

262. <u>1893</u>

Utah. Hunt & Eaton. New York. L. B. Folger Sr. Cin.

29 x 23 cm. colored, 1:2,400,000.

Colored by counties. Boundaries current to 1890.
Railroads to Frisco, Stockton, Manti, Tintic, and Scofield.

<u>The Columbian Atlas of the World We Live In</u>. New York,
Hunt & Eaton, 1893.

Phillips 981.

UHS, LC.

263. <u>1893</u>

     Indexed Atlas of the World. [Utah] Rand, McNally & Co.'s New Business Atlas Map of Utah. Copyright 1893 by Rand, McNally & Co.

     48 x 32 cm. colored, 1:1,457,000.

     Colored by counties with boundaries current. Shows railroads to Frisco, Marysville, and Mud Creek (Clear Creek).

     <u>Rand, McNally & Co.'s Indexed Atlas of the World</u>. Chicago, Rand, McNally, page 431.

     SLP.

264. <u>1893</u>

     Territory of Utah. 1893. Compiled from the Official Records of the General Land Office and other sources under supervision of Harry King C. E. . . . . Photo lith. & print by Forbes Co. Boston & N. Y. Compiled and drawn by R.H. Morton. Lettered by M. Hendges.

     92 x 72 cm. colored, 1:760,320.

     Shows township section lines, roads, and railroads, including a spur to "New Wales" (Winter Quarters). Relief shown by hill shading.

     Hargett 791; Phillips p949; Phillips 11047.

     LDSH, BYU, UU, GSL, SLP, UHS, LC.

265. <u>1893</u>

     Utah.

     30 x 23 cm., 1:2,300,000.

Grand County is not shown. Looks like a Cram or a Rand, McNally map. Page 89 of a Gaskill atlas, Chicago, 1893.

BYU.

266. <u>1893</u>

Utah—Col. Abajo Sheet. U. S. Geological Survey. Henry Gannet, Chief Geographer. A. H. Thompson, Geographer in charge. Triangulation by A. P. Davis. Topography by the U. S. Geological and Hayden Surveys. Edition of June 1893.

45 x 36 cm. colored, 1:250,000.

Relief shown by contours, contour interval 250 feet. Shows from 37° N. to 38° N. and from 109° W. to 110° W. Surveyed in 1884.

LDSH, UHS, BYU, USU, LC.

267. <u>1893</u>

Map of American Fork City, Utah County, Utah. Compiled from Surveys to J. Fewson Smith Jr. 1893.

36 x 45 cm., 1:7,200 or 600 ft to 1 inch.

Original drawing was at the scale of 200 feet to 1 inch. Notes and certificate on left margin. Signed by J. Fewson Smith, Jr. Accepted as the official map of the city July ____ 1893 by _____ Chipman, Mayor, George F. Shelley, City Recorder. Lots are numbered.

BYU.

268. <u>1893</u>

Map of Salt Lake City showing business portion and, more important, residential district. This map shows the most important lines of the Salt Lake City Railroad Company. Published by E. H.

Rollins & Sons, Bankers, No. 33 Wall Street, New York City, by permission of Messrs. Browne & Brooks, of Salt Lake City, Utah. Korff Bros. & Co., 161 Washington St., N. Y.

25 x 40 cm. colored, scale not given.

Based on the 1888 Browne & Brooks plat. Shows blocks, lots, with wards numbered, important buildings named, constructed lines in red, proposed lines in yellow. Investment information on verso.

LDSH.

269. <u>1894</u>

Rand, McNally & Co.'s Utah. Rand, McNally & Co.'s New Business Atlas Map of Utah. Copyright 1893. by Rand, McNally & Co., Map Publishers and Engravers, Chicago, 1894.

48 x 32 cm. colored, 1:1,457,280 or 23 miles to 1 inch.

Colored by counties. Carbon County is not shown. Antimony is called "Coyoto."

Phillips p949.

BYU, LC.

270. <u>1894</u>

Kaysville, Davis Co., Utah. July 1894. Sanborn Map Company, New York.

1 sheet, 64 x 54 cm. colored, 1:600.

Shows from 6th St. to 8th St. and from Cherry to Locust, plus Kaysville Mill & Elevator Co.

UU.

271. <u>1895</u>

Relief Map of Utah. 1895. Drawn by Mosiah Hall . . .
assisted by Charles Wright . . . Location of minerals carefully
corrected by Don Maguire . . . Copyright 1895 by Mosiah Hall.
Published by Pierce & McMillen, Salt Lake City. Salt Lake Lithographing Co.

126 x 96 cm. colored, 1:475,200 or "7½ miles to the inch."
Relief drawn in a hachure style of continuous horizontal
views. Names of mineral resources overprinted in red.

Phillips p949.

USU, BYU, LC.

272. <u>1895</u>

Rand, McNally & Co.'s Utah. Rand, McNally & Co.'s New
Business Atlas of Utah. Copyright 1893 by Rand, McNally & Co.
Rand, McNally & Co. Map Publishers and Engravers, Chicago, 1895.

48 x 32 cm. colored, 1:1,450,000.

Colored by counties. Shows Carbon County. County lines,
state lines, and list of railroads overprinted in red.

Phillips 1001.

LDSH, LC.

273. <u>1895</u>

[Utah] Atlas of the World. Rand, McNally & Co.'s New
11 x 14 Map of Utah. Copyright, 1895, by Rand, McNally & Co.

31 x 23 cm. colored, 1:2,000,000.

Colored by counties. List of cities down both sides.

Rand, McNally & Co.'s Unrivaled Atlas of the World.
Chicago, Rand, McNally, 1900, page 64.

Another copy is page cv in Standard Atlas of the World.
New York, Funk & Wagnalls, 1896.

Phillips 1008.

Another copy titled "Map of the State of Utah, 1896"
printed above a calendar with list of towns with population down both
sides and population of precincts by county on the verso.

WCL, LDSH, UHS, LC.

274. 1896

Rand, McNally & Co.'s Utah. Rand, McNally & Co.'s New
Business Atlas Map of Utah, Copyright, 1895 by Rand, McNally & Co.
Rand, McNally & Co., Map Publishers and Engravers, 1896.

48 x 32 cm. colored, 1:1,450,000.

County lines, state lines, and a list of railroads overprinted in red. List of towns down left side.

LDSH.

275. 1896

Utah Fish Lake Sheet. U.S. Geological Survey. Triangulation
and Topography by the Powell Survey. Edition of July 1896.

45 x 35 cm. colored, 1:250,000.

Shows from 38° N. to 39° N. and from 110° W. to 112° W.
Relief shown by contours, contour interval 250 feet. Surveyed in
1885. Reprinted Jan. 1899.

LDSH, USU, BYU, LC.

276. <u>1896</u>

Mount Pleasant, Sanpete Co., Utah. Aug. 1896. Sanborn
Map Company, New York.

5 sheets 64 x 54 cm. colored, 1:600.

Shows from 1st to 8th and from E to I Streets, plus Mount
Pleasant Roller Mill Co.

UU, LC.

277. <u>1897</u>

The Century Atlas Nevada and Utah. Copyright 1897 by The
Century Co., New York. The Matthews-Northrup Co., Buffalo, N. Y.

37 x 27 cm. colored, 1:2,979,920 or "Scale 47 English
statute Miles to One Inch."

Shows township lines, railroad, and post routes. Relief
shown by hachures and by contour lines at 1,000 foot intervals. Inset
of Salt Lake area from Pleasant Grove to North Ogden in lower left,
"Scale, 16 Miles to One Inch," 1:1,013,760.

<u>The Century Atlas of the World</u>. New York, Century, 1897.
No. 54

Phillips 1020.

WCL, UHS, LDSH, BYU, LC.

278. <u>1897</u>

Post Route Map of the State of Utah Showing Post Offices
with Intermediate Distances on Mail Routes in Operation on the 1st
of December, 1897. Published by order of the Postmaster General James
A. Grey under the direction of A. von Haake, Topographer, P. O.
Dept., Washington, 1897.

103 x 74 cm.

Shows post offices, mail routes, and frequency of delivery.

Phillips p950.

LC.

279. <u>1897</u>

Utah Tintic Mining District. U.S. Geological Survey.
R. U. Goode, Geographer in charge. Triangulation by S. S. Gannett.
Topography by W. T. Griswold and R. B. Marshall.

77 x 45 cm. colored, 1:9,600.

Relief shown by contours, 20 foot interval. Shows from
39°54' N. to 39°08" N. and from 112°05'30" W. to 112°08'30" W.
Major mines named.

Another edition overprinted to show "Economic Geology Sheet"
with three profiles. Another edition revised by R. B. Marshall,
Aug. 1898. Topographic and geologic editions published in <u>Geologic</u>
<u>Atlas of the United States. Tintic Special Folio</u>, Utah. U.S.
Geological Survey Folio 65. 1900.

USU, UU, BYU, LC.

280. <u>1898</u>

Froiseth's New Sectional & Mineral Map of Utah. Compiled
from the latest U.S. Government Surveys and other authentic sources
Exhibiting the Sections, Townships, Ranges, Counties, Cities, Towns,
Settlements, Mining Districts, and other Internal Improvements.
Designed for use in Schools, Colleges, Libraries, and Business
Houses. Published under the Patronage of the State Legislature by

B. A. M. Froiseth C. E., Salt Lake City, 1898. Drawn & printed by
W. B. Walkup & Co. Map Publishers, San Francisco, Cal.

164 x 124 cm., 1:380,160 or 6 miles to 1 inch.

Along the upper margin are seven photos of schools and
colleges. Diagrams show judicial districts, U.S. survey system, and
a list of mining districts.

UU, BYU.

281. 1898

Post Route Map of the State of Utah, Showing Post Offices
with Intermediate Distances on Mail Routes in Operation on the 1st
of December, 1898. Published by order of Postmaster General Charles
Emory Smith Under the direction of A. von Haake, Topographer. P. O.
Dept., Washington, 1898.

104 x 74 cm.

Shows post offices and mail routes with frequency of delivery.

Phillips p950.

LC.

282. 1898

Utah.

34 x 26 cm. colored, 1:1,800,000.

Colored by counties with current boundaries.

Page 87 of a Cram atlas.

BYU.

283. <u>1898</u>

Bingham West Mountain Mining District, Salt Lake County,
Utah. Compiled for the Bingham Bulletin from official records in the
office of U.S. Surveyor General. Under the direction of (signed)
J. Fewson Smith. Lithographed by the Utah Lithographing Company,
Salt Lake City.

77 x 62 cm., 1:14,400 or 1,200 feet to 1 inch.

Shows mining claims and railroads.

LDSH, SLP.

284. <u>1898</u>

Utah Tintic Special Sheet. U.S. Geological Survey.

Edition of July 1898. R. U. Goode, Geographer in charge.
Triangulation by S. S. Gannett. Topography by R. B. Marshall.
Surveyed in 1897.

45 x 35 cm. colored, 1:62,500.

Relief shown by contours at 50 foot intervals. Shows from
$39^{o}45'$ N. to 40° N. and from $111^{o}55'$ W. to $112^{o}10'$W.

"Historical Geology Sheet" and "Structure--Section Sheet"
published with topographic edition in <u>Geologic Atlas of the United
States. Tintic Special Folio, Utah</u>. U.S. Geological Survey Folio
65. 1900.

LDSH, UHS, USU, BYU, UU, LC.

285. <u>1898</u>

Map of Salt Lake City and vicinity compiled and drawn for
The Midland Investment Co. Real Estate, Loans and Investments. 177
Main Street, Salt Lake City, Utah.

71 x 46 cm., 1:325,000.

Insets of "Map of Intermountain Region" and map of western U.S. railroads. Description on verso.

BYU.

286. <u>1898</u>

Bingham Canyon, Salt Lake Co., Utah. July 1898. Sanborn Map Company, New York.

5 sheets, 64 x 54 cm. colored, 1:600.

Shows Main St. and Carr's Fork; plus North Last Chance M'g. Co.'s Concentrator, Dalton and Lark Gold, Silver and Lead Mill and Mining Co.'s Plant, Lead Mine Hoisting Works, Brooklyn Mine Hoisting Works, Yosemite No. 2 Hoisting Works, Highland Boy Gold Mining Co., Yosemite No. 1 Hoisting Works, Old Jordan and Galena Mining Co., Nigara Silver M'g. Co.'s Concentrator, South Galena M. and M. Co., Bevan M. and M. Co.'s Gold Mill.

UU, LC.

287. <u>1898</u>

Corinne, Box Elder Co., Utah. May 1898. Sanborn Map Company, New York.

3 sheets, 64 x 54 cm. colored, 1:600.

Shows from 8th St. to 2nd St. and from Washington St. to Arizona St., plus Corinne Roller Mills.

UU, LC.

288. <u>1898</u>

Ephraim, San Pete Co., Utah. Aug. 1898. Sanborn Map Company, New York.

2 sheets, 64 x 54 cm. colored, 1:600.

Shows from Main St. to A. East and from 2nd North St. to 2nd South St., plus Climax Roller Mills.

UU, LC.

289. <u>1898</u>

Eureka, Juab Co., Utah. Aug. 1898. Sanborn Map Company, New York.

6 sheets, 64 x 54 cm. colored, 1:600.

Shows two or three blocks on either side of Main St., plus Centennial Eureka Mining Co., Bullion Beck & Champion Mining Co.'s Hoist, Eureka Hill Mining Co. Hoisting Works, Eureka Hill Mining Co.'s Mill, Bullion Beck & Champion Mining Co.'s Mill.

UU, LC.

290. <u>1898</u>

Lehi, Utah Co., Utah. July 1898. Sanborn Map Company, New York.

7 sheets, 64 x 54 cm. colored, 1:600.

Shows from 5th West to 2nd East and from the Oregon Short Line Railroad to 2nd South, plus Utah Sugar Company's Plant.

UU, LC.

291. <u>1898</u>

Mammoth, Juab Co., Utah.   Sept. 1898.   Sanborn Map Company, New York.

3 sheets, 64 x 54 cm. colored, 1:600.

Shows both Mammoth Hollow and Robinson.

UU, LC.

292. <u>1898</u>

Mercur, Tooele Co., Utah.   Aug. 1898.   Sanborn Map Company, New York.

6 sheets, 64 x 54 cm. colored, 1:600.

Includes Manning, Sunshine, and West Dip.   Shows two or three blocks on either side of Main and Geyser, plus Geyser-Marion Mining Co.'s "Geyser Mill," DeLamar Mercur Mines Co. "Golden Gate Mill," Chloride Point Con. Mining Co., Boston & Mercur Gold Mining Co.'s "La Cigale Mill," Mercur Gold Mining & Milling Co.'s "Mattie" Hoist, Sacramento Gold Mining & Milling Co., Northern Light Mining & Milling Co., Overland Gold Mining & Milling Co., Sunshine Gold Mining & Milling Co., Daisy Mining Co., Mercur Gold Mining & Milling Co.'s Mill.

UU, LC.

293. <u>1898</u>

Salt Lake City, Salt Lake Co., Utah.   1898.   Sanborn Map Company, New York.

187 sheets, 64 x 54 cm. colored, 1:600.

Includes Murray, Sandy, Garfield Beach, Taylorsville, and Saltair, plus many insets of commercial and industrial establishments outside the built-up area.

UU, LC.

294. <u>1898</u>

Springville, Utah Co., Utah. July 1898. Sanborn Map Company, New York.

7 sheets, 64 x 54 cm. colored, 1:600.

Shows from 5th to 10th and from Adams to below Grant, plus the Public School and Elders Hall, Springville Milling Co., Springville Woolen Mills.

UU, LC.

295. <u>1899</u>

Utah. Bradley & Poates.

13 x 9 cm, 1:5,700,000.

No county lines.

Published by The Bradstreet Co., N.Y.

BYU.

296. <u>1899</u>

Prospectors' Map of Utah. Poole Bro., Engravers, Chicago.

Mining districts numbered and listed on the left. Logo of the Rio Grande Western Railroad in the upper right. List of agents along the lower left and bottom. Shows roads and railroads, existing and projected.

Issued with <u>History of Utah's Great Mining Districts</u> by
Don Maguire, 1899. Another copy is included in a brochure titled
"The Prospectors' Map of Utah showing all mining districts of record,
with an outline sketch of those which have achieved renown, while
others give promise of bustling life during the season of 1897." Utah
Mining Series No. 3.

     LDSH, UU.

297. <u>1899</u>

     Poste Route Map of the State of Utah showing post offices
with the intermediate distances on mail routes in operation on the
1st of March 1899. Published by order of Postmaster General Charles
Emory Smith under the direction of A. von Haake, Topographer P.O.
Dept.

     104 x 74 cm.

     Shows counties, post offices, roads, railroads, distances
between towns and frequency of delivery.

     Phillips p950.

     GSL, SLP, BYU, LC.

298. <u>1899</u>

     Soil Map. Salt Lake Sheet. U.S. Dept. of Agriculture.
Division of Soils . . . Utah Agricultural Experiment Station . . .
Surveyed by Frank A. Gardner and John Stewart 1899. Edition of 1899.
Lith. by A. Hoen & Co. Baltimore, Md. Scale 1 inch = 1 mile. H.
Doc. 399561.

     76 x 43 cm. colored, 1:63,360.

Shows soil classes by color for the area on the west side of the Jordan River from Bluffdale to its mouth. Shows railroads, canals, township and section lines, and city street grids.

Other editions colored to show underground water and alkalai.

Published with U.S. Dept. of Agriculture. Report No. 64. Field Operations of the Division of Soils. Washington, G. P. O., 1900. Superintendent of Documents #A26.5:899.

BYU, LDSH, USU, UU, LC.

299. 1899

Bingham, West Mountain Mining District, U. Compiled and drawn by Charles Mostyn Owen.

48 x 39 cm., 1:16,920.

Shows and names mining claims, roads, railroads, and some buildings. Seal of Rio Grande Western Railway in the upper left.

Accompanies Outline History of Utah's Great Mining Districts by Don Maguire.

UU, UHS.

300. 1899

Mercur. Map of Camp Floyd Mining District and West Dip, Utah. Compiled and drawn by Charles Mostyn Owen.

58 x 74 cm., 1:21,600.

Shows sections, mining claims, railroads, townsites, mills, and the Rio Grande Western Railway logo.

UU, UHS.

301. <u>1899</u>

Mercur, Utah's Johannesburg. Compiled from official records and other sources. Published by W. M. Wantland. Salt Lake City, Utah, March 15, 1899.

87 x 56 cm., 1:23,470.

Shows sections, mining claims, railroads. Includes eleven photos and advertisements from Union Pacific Railroad and Salt Lake Stock and Mining Exchange. Lists mining stocks, dividend paying mines, promising dividend payers, and meritorious prospects.

LDSH, UHS.

302. <u>1899</u>

Tintic Mining District, Utah. Compiled and Drawn by Charles Mostyn Owen C.E. Salt Lake City, U. Mar. 1899.

32 x 65 cm.

Oriented with east at the top and Rio Grande Western Railway logo on the right. Shows city blocks, railroads, and mining claims.

UU, BYU.

303. <u>1899</u>

Map of Fish Lake Forest Reserve situated in Sevier, Piute, and Wayne Counties, Utah as created by Proclamation of February 10th 1899. U.S. Surveyor General's Office, Salt Lake City, Utah. May 15th 1899 (signed) Jacob B. Blair, U.S. Surveyor General.

39 x 23 cm., 1:126,720 or "Scale 2 miles to one inch."

Shows sections, roads, and cabins.

BYU.

Bibliography

Allen, James B. "The Evolution of County Boundaries in Utah."
    Utah Historical Quarterly, 23:261-278, July, 1955.

Alter, J. Cecil. "Father Escalante's Map." Utah Historical Quar-
    terly, 9:64-72, January-April, 1941.

American Geographical Society. Map Department Index to Maps in
    Books and Periodicals. 10 vols. plus 2 supplements. Boston:
    G. K. Hall, 1968-1976.

American Library Association. Resources and Technical Service
    Division. The National Union Catalog; Pre-1956 Imprints.
    ca. 680 vols. London: Mansel, 1968-   .

The Bancroft Library, University of California, Berkeley. Index
    to Printed Maps. 1 vol. plus supplement. Boston: G. K. Hall,
    1964.

Bartlett, Richard A. Great Surveys of the American West. Norman,
    Oklahoma: University of Oklahoma Press, 1962.

Briggs, Walter. Without Noise of Arms. Flagstaff, Arizona: North-
    land Press, 1976.

Checklist of United States Public Documents, 1789-1909. 3rd ed.
    Washington, D.C.: U.S. Government Printing Office, 1911.

Cobb, David Alan. "Vermont Maps Prior to 1900: An Annotated Carto-
    bibliography." Vermont History, 39:384, 1971.

Crampton, C. Gregory. "Humboldt's Utah, 1811." Utah Historical
    Quarterly, 26:268-281, July, 1958.

Day, James M. Maps of Texas 1527-1900: The Map Collection of the
    Texas State Archives. Austin, Texas: Pemberton Press, 1964.

Fremont, John Charles. Memoirs of My Life. Chicago: Bedford,
    Clarke & Co., 1887.

Goetzman, William H. Army Exploration in the American West, 1803-
    1863. New Haven, Connecticut: Yale University Press, 1959.

Hargett, Janet L. List of Selected Maps of States and Territories.
    (Special List No. 29.) Washington, D.C.: U.S. National Arch-
    ives, 1971.

Hébert, John R. Panoramic Maps of Anglo-American Cities: A Check-
    list of Maps in the Collections of the Library of Congress,
    Geography and Map Division. Washington, D.C.: Library of
    Congress, 1974.

Jackson, Richard H. Myth and Reality: Environmental Perceptions of
    the Mormons, 1840-1865: An Historical Geosophy. (Ph.D. Dis-
    sertation.) Worcester, Massachusetts: Clark University, 1970.

Kelsay, Laura E. List of Cartographic Records of the General Land
    Office. (Special List No. 19) Washington, D.C.: U.S. Na-
    tional Archives.

Ladd, Richard S. Maps Showing Explorers' Routes, Trails, and Early
    Roads in the United States: An Annotated List. Washington,
    D.C.: Library of Congress, Map Division, Reference Department,
    1962.

LeGear, Clara Egli. United States Atlases: A List of National,
    State, County, City, and Regional Atlases in the Library of
    Congress. 2 vols. Washington, D.C.: The Library of Congress,
    Reference Department, 1950-1953.

Lister, Raymond. How to Identify Old Maps and Globes, With a List
    of Cartographers, Engravers, Publishers, and Printers Concerned
    With Printed Maps and Globes from c. 1500 to c. 1850. Hamden:
    Archon Books, 1965.

Lowery, Woodbury. A Descriptive List of Maps of the Spanish Posses-
    sions Within the Present Limits of the United States, 1502-1820.
    Washington, D.C.: U.S. Government Printing Office, 1912.

Malone, Dumas, ed. Dictionary of American Biography. 20 vols.
    New York: Charles Scribner's Sons, 1933.

Marshall, Douglas W., ed. Research Catalog of Maps of America to
    1860 in the William L. Clements Library, University of Michigan,
    Ann Arbor, Michigan. 4 vols. Boston: G. K. Hall, 1972.

Mason, Sara Elizabeth. A List of Nineteenth Century Maps of the
    State of Alabama. Birmingham: Birmingham Public Library, 1973.

Miller, David E. Utah History Atlas. Salt Lake City: David E.
    Miller, 1979.

Morgan, Dale Lowell. The Great Salt Lake. Indianapolis, Indiana:
    Bobbs-Merrill, 1947.

Morgan, Dale L., & Carl I. Wheat. Jedediah Smith and His Maps of
    the American West. San Francisco: California Historical So-
    ciety, 1952.

Phillips, Philip Lee, & Clara Egli LeGear. A List of Geographical Atlases in the Library of Congress with Bibliographic Notes. 8 vols. Washington, D.C.: U.S. Government Printing Office, 1909-1974.

Phillips, Philip Lee. A List of Maps of America in the Library of Congress. Washington, D.C.: Government Printing Office, 1901.

Rabbitt, Mary C. Minerals, Lands, and Geology for the Common Defense and General Welfare. Volume 1: Before 1879. Washington, D.C.: U.S. Government Printing Office, 1979.

Reps, John W. Cities of the American West: A History of Frontier Urban Planning. Princeton, New Jersey: Princeton University Press, 1979.

Ristow, Walter William. Maps for an Emerging Nation: Commercial Cartography in Nineteenth-Century America. Washington, D.C.: Library of Congress, 1977.

Ristow, Walter William. "United States Fire Insurance and Underwriters Maps, 1852-1968." Quarterly Journal of the Library of Congress, 25:194-218, July, 1968.

Sames, James W. III, & Lewis C. Woods, Jr. Index of Kentucky and Virginia Maps, 1562 to 1900. Frankfort, Kentucky: Kentucky Historical Society, 1976.

Schmeckebier, L. F. Catalogue and Index to the Publications of the Hayden, King, Powell, and Wheeler Surveys. (U.S. Geological Survey Bulletin, No. 222.) Washington, D.C.: U. S. Government Printing Office, 1904.

Seavey, Charles. "Wheat to Serial Set Conversion Chart." Special Libraries Association Geography and Map Division Bulletin, 108:37-40, June, 1977.

Stephenson, Richard W. Land Ownership Maps: A Checklist of Nineteenth Century United States County Maps in the Library of Congress. Washington, D.C.: Library of Congress, 1967.

Tooley, Ronald Vere. Tooley's Dictionary of Mapmakers. New York: Alan R. Liss, 1979.

United States Geographical Surveys West of the One Hundredth Meridian in Charge of Capt. Geo. M. Wheeler, Corps of Engineers, U.S. Army Under the Direction of the Chief of Engineers, U.S. Army. Vol. 1: Geographical Report. Washington, D.C.: U.S. Government Printing Office, 1889.

U.S. Army Engineer Department. List of Reports and Maps of the United States Geographical Surveys West of the 100th Meridian. George M. Wheeler, Captain, Corps of Engineers, U.S. Army, in Charge. 2nd ed. Washington, D.C.: U.S. Government Printing Office, 1881.

U.S. War Department. Reports of Explorations and Surveys to Ascer-
     tain the Most Practicable and Economical Route for a Railroad
     from the Mississippi River to the Pacific Ocean. Made Under the
     Direction of the Secretary of War, in 1853-6. Washington, D.C.:
     33rd Congress, 2nd Session. Senate Ex. Doc. No. 78, Vol. 11.

VanCott, John W. Geographic Names of Utah: A Compilation.
     forthcoming.

Warren, Gouverneur Kemble. Memoir to Accompany the Map of the Ter-
     ritory of the United States from the Mississippi River to the
     Pacific Ocean. Washington, D.C.: Beverly Tucker, 1859.

Wheat, Carl Irving. Mapping the Transmississippi West. 5 vols. in
     6. San Francisco: The Institute of Historical Cartography,
     1957-1963.

Index

Adlard, H., 63
Alta, 110,116
American Fork, 236,267
Appleton, D. & Co., 46
Asher & Adams, 114,115

Bancroft, A.L., 137
Bancroft, Hubert Howe, 69, 73,
  74, 81, 83, 90, 92, 93, 104,
  107
Bartholomew, John, 41, 119
Bartlett, John R., 31
Beadle, 101
Bear River Valley, 232
Beckwith, Edward Griffin, 34,
  35, 36, 37
Biedermann, E., 28
Bingham Canyon, 237, 283, 286,
  299
Bishop, F. M., 120
Black, Adam & Charles, 41
Bonneville, Benjamin Louis
  Eulalie de, 5, 6, 32
Bradley, William M., 182, 208,
  211, 222
Bradley & Poates, 295
Bradstreet Co., 295
Brigham City, 131, 135, 186,
  238
Browne & Brooks, 219, 268
Brué, Adrien Hubert, 4
Bullock, Thomas, 63
Burns, John L., 109
Burr, David H., 8, 44, 45
Burroughs, H. N., 14, 21, 22
Burton, Richard F., 63

Carrington, Albert, 25, 26
Century Co., 277
Chittenden, Hiram, 220
Clark, Charles Russell, 83
Coalville, 131
Colby, Charles B., 50
Colton, George Woolworth, 89, 96, 112,
  122, 143, 156
Colton, Joseph Hutchins, 19, 31, 32,
  19, 64, 67, 70, 75, 76, 77, 78
Corinne, 111, 131, 136, 187, 232,
  239, 287
Cowperthwait, Huling, 21, 22, 24, 29
Cram, George Franklin, 157, 176, 177,
  183, 212, 250, 251, 258, 282
Crofutt, George A., 108, 192

Darke, Sydney W., 214
Darling, Eugene F., 224
Day (John) & Sons, 33, 51, 68
DeMotte, H., 120
Desilver, Charles, 29, 42
Dewerthen, H., 98
Dimmock, C. H., 61
Dinsmore, A. F., 186, 223
Disturnell, John, 15, 18, 30
Dodge, Grenville, M., 99
Dougal, W. H., 60
DuBois, N., 86
DuPuy, W. H., 210
Durkee, H. R., 110
Dutton, Clarence Edward, 158,
  159, 160, 161, 170, 171, 172,
  173

NOTE: All index entries refer to Map Numbers in Chapters II - VII.

NOTE: All index entries refer to Map Numbers in Chapters II - VII.

NOTE: All index entries refer to Map Numbers in Chapters II - VII.

_____

NOTE: All index entries refer to Map Numbers in Chapters II - VII.

Other Publications from the
WESTERN ASSOCIATION OF MAP LIBRARIES

The **Information Bulletin** is the principal publication of WAML. Begun in 1969, and issued three times each year, the **Information Bulletin** is available on a Volume Year basis only. Mid-year subscribers or new Members receive back issues for the Volume Year, which begins July 1. Full sets of earlier volumes are also available. (LC # 72-625238; ISSN 0049-7282). A cumulative index to the first ten volumes is in preparation.

Occasional Paper No. 1: *Catalog of Sanborn Atlases at California State University, Northridge,* by Gary W. Rees and Mary Hoeber. 1973. xxi, 122p. (LC # 73-5773; ISBN 0-939112-01-9) $4.00

Occasional Paper No. 2: *Union List of Sanborn Fire Insurance Maps Held by Institutions in the United States and Canada, Vol. 1, Alabama to Missouri,* by R. Philip Hoehn. 1976. xvii, 178p. (LC # 76-6129; ISBN 0-939112-02-7) $5.00

Occasional Paper No. 3: *Union List of Sanborn Fire Insurance Maps Held by Institutions in the United States and Canada, Vol. 2, Montana to Wyoming; Canada and Mexico,* by William S. Peterson-Hunt and Evelyn L. Woodruff; *with a Supplement and Corrigenda to Volume 1,* by R. Philip Hoehn. 1977. xv, 201p. (LC # 76-6129 Rev.; ISBN 0-939112-03-5) $6.00

Occasional Papers No. 2 and No. 3 (when ordered together) (ISBN 0-939112-04-3) $10.00

Occasional Paper No. 4: *Index to early twentieth century city plans appearing in guidebooks: Baedeker, Muirhead-Blue Guides, Murray, I.J.G.R., etc., plus selected other works to provide worldwide coverage of over 2,000 plans to over 1,200 communities, found in 74 guidebooks,* by Harold M. Otness. 1978. xxx, 94p. (LC # 78-15094; ISBN 0-939112-05-1) $6.00

Occasional Paper No. 5: *The Maps of Fiji: a selective and annotated cartobibliography,* by Mason S. Green. 1978. xx, 70p. (LC # 78-24066; ISBN 0-939112-06-X) $4.00

Occasional Paper No. 6: *Microcartography: applications for archives and libraries,* edited by Larry Cruse, with the assistance of Sylvia B. Warren. (in preparation) (ISBN 0-939112-07-8)

Occasional Paper No. 7: *Index to nineteenth century city plans appearing in guidebooks: Baedeker, Murray, Joanne, Black, Appleton, Meyer, plus selected other works to provide coverage of over 1,800 plans to nearly 600 communities, found in 164 guidebooks,* by Harold M. Otness. 1980. xxiv, 84p. (LC # 80-24483; ISBN 0-939112-08-6) $6.00

Occasional Paper No. 8: *Printed Maps of Utah before 1800; an annotated cartobibliography,* by Riley Moore Moffat. 1981. xvi, 177p. (LC # 81-659; ISBN 0-939112-09-4) $10.00

Subscriptions to the Information Bulletin, standing orders for the OP series, or single items may be ordered from: Western Association of Map Libraries, c/o Stanley D. Stevens, Treasurer, University Library, University of California, Santa Cruz, CA 95064.